Managing Global Debt

A Staff Paper by
Richard S. Dale and Richard P. Mattione

THE BROOKINGS INSTITUTION
Washington, D.C.

© *1983 by*
THE BROOKINGS INSTITUTION
1775 Massachusetts Avenue, N.W., Washington, D.C. 20036

Library of Congress Catalog Card Number 83-72567

ISBN 0-8157-1717-2

1 2 3 4 5 6 7 8 9

THE BROOKINGS INSTITUTION is an independent organization devoted to nonpartisan research, education, and publication in economics, government, foreign policy, and the social sciences generally. Its principal purposes are to aid in the development of sound public policies and to promote public understanding of issues of national importance.

The Institution was founded on December 8, 1927, to merge the activities of the Institute for Government Research, founded in 1916, the Institute of Economics, founded in 1922, and the Robert Brookings Graduate School of Economics and Government, founded in 1924.

The Board of Trustees is responsible for the general administration of the Institution, while the immediate direction of the policies, program, and staff is vested in the President, assisted by an advisory committee of the officers and staff. The by-laws of the Institution state: "It is the function of the Trustees to make possible the conduct of scientific research, and publication, under the most favorable conditions, and to safeguard the independence of the research staff in the pursuit of their studies and in the publication of the results of such studies. It is not a part of their function to determine, control, or influence the conduct of particular investigations or the conclusions reached."

The President bears final responsibility for the decision to publish a manuscript as a Brookings book. In reaching his judgment on the competence, accuracy, and objectivity of each study, the President is advised by the director of the appropriate research program and weighs the views of a panel of expert outside readers who report to him in confidence on the quality of the work. Publication of a work signifies that it is deemed a competent treatment worthy of public consideration but does not imply endorsement of conclusions or recommendations.

The Institution maintains its position of neutrality on issues of public policy in order to safeguard the intellectual freedom of the staff. Hence interpretations or conclusions in Brookings publications should be understood to be solely those of the authors and should not be attributed to the Institution, to its trustees, officers, or other staff members, or to the organizations that support its research.

Foreword

EVENTS of the last eighteen months have raised serious concerns about the buildup of international debt. The Polish crisis, war in the Falkland Islands, and Mexico's widely publicized financial troubles caused a sudden reappraisal of commercial bank lending to developing countries. Isolated financial problems were transformed into a more generalized debt crisis. As a result, Western governments, commercial banks, the International Monetary Fund, and borrowing countries have become engaged in complex negotiations designed to resolve, or at least to smooth over, the current debt problems. In the background has been the fear that, because of global economic interdependence, a failure to reach an accommodation could threaten the stability of world economic relationships more generally.

In this study Richard S. Dale and Richard P. Mattione focus on two sets of issues. They argue first that emergency lending facilities and procedures must be adequate to deal with the current debt crisis, and second that ways must be found to reduce the likelihood of similar problems in the future. They conclude that economic growth alone will not meet these twin goals; changes in the design of the international financial system will be needed.

Richard S. Dale was a guest scholar in the Economic Studies program at Brookings at the time this staff paper was written. His work at Brookings was made possible by an international relations fellowship from the Rockefeller Foundation. Richard P. Mattione is a research associate in the Brookings Foreign Policy Studies program. The authors are grateful to Edward M. Bernstein, Ralph C. Bryant, Michael Dooley, Jack Guttentag, Richard Herring, Peter B. Kenen, Lawrence B. Krause, Sam Pizer, Walter S. Salant, Robert Solomon, John D. Steinbruner, and Edwin M. Truman for helpful comments and suggestions. They are also grateful to Virginia R. Black, who typed many drafts; to Jean Rosenblatt, who edited the manuscript; and to Christine Potts, who verified its factual content.

The study was funded by grants from the Ford Foundation, the German Marshall Fund of the United States, the Rockefeller Foundation, and the National Science Foundation.

The views expressed are those of the authors and should not be ascribed to the organizations whose assistance is acknowledged above or to the trustees, officers, or other staff members of the Brookings Institution.

BRUCE K. MACLAURY
President

August 1983
Washington, D.C.

To establish a sounder foundation for foreign lending in future is therefore one of the two or three most important reforms the world needs, if a recurrence of our present troubles is to be avoided.

ARTHUR S. SALTER, 1932

THE ISSUE of global debt has emerged once again, during economic and financial conditions uncomfortably similar to those of the 1930s. While bank lending to developing countries increased at an annual rate of 20 to 25 percent throughout the mid-1970s and early 1980s, such lending came to an abrupt halt in mid-1982 as bankers' confidence evaporated in the wake of Mexico's financial difficulties.[1] This sudden interruption in the flow of credit threatened to precipitate a number of defaults, since without new money major borrowers would be unable to pay interest— let alone principal—on their existing loans.[2] To avert this danger national authorities, along with the International Monetary Fund (IMF), have orchestrated a series of emergency credit programs. Under this regime banks have been required to commit additional funds to problem borrowers according to a quota allocation system, which has used as its benchmark each bank's exposure to the country concerned. Such a response to the financial crisis recognizes that, temporarily at least, the market mechanism has failed.

International Lending before and after World War II

The history of international lending in the nineteenth and twentieth centuries contains numerous incidents of default. The last series of

---

1. These growth rates were achieved despite occasional reschedulings of commercial credits. But even the largest reschedulings of the 1970s (for Peru and Turkey) involved only $3.5 billion to $4 billion in bank debt.

2. The term *default* can apply to a variety of debt-servicing interruptions, ranging from formal repudiation to a unilateral suspension of principal or interest payments. Default may be de facto or, when declared by creditors, de jure. Suspension of interest payments is particularly serious for banks because they lose the interest income and therefore incur losses.

1

widespread defaults—before 1982—occurred in the 1930s, when most Eastern European and Latin American borrowers suspended payments because of financial difficulties triggered by the Great Depression. Understanding the international lending arrangements that contributed to those defaults helps clarify current debt problems.

A key feature of prewar credit markets was the predominant role of bond finance. Bonds were usually issued at fixed rates of interest with long periods until maturity. Furthermore, banks usually did not extend their own funds to foreign borrowers but merely served as underwriters and promoters of bond issues that were purchased by individual investors. Bank assets were not normally at risk, therefore, when debt servicing problems arose.

One consequence of this financing method was that creditors (that is, bondholders) were not well placed to negotiate reschedulings. Instead, debtor countries experiencing financial strains would typically suspend payments for a time and, when they wanted access to credit markets again, would try to negotiate partial relief on their old debt. The terms of bond issues, however, seem to have anticipated such difficulties: the bonds were often issued at steep discounts from face value, and the contracted interest rates far exceeded rates on "risk-free" investments such as British government bonds.

Debt-servicing problems often accompanied recessions. Economists surveying the defaults of the 1930s, for example, found certain similarities with events of the nineteenth century, when "every major downward swing of the business cycle caused the failure of governments and other foreign borrowers to meet their external obligations."[3] But recessions were not the sole cause of defaults in the 1930s. In particular, a deterioration in the quality of new issues during the 1920s seems also to have been a factor.[4]

Whatever the cause of the defaults, private bondholder committees carried the burden of loan renegotiations and were backed by the threat

3. John T. Madden, Marcus Nadler, and Harry C. Sauvain, *America's Experience as a Creditor Nation* (Prentice-Hall, 1937), p. 107.

4. The quality (as measured by their payments status in 1937) of bond issues deteriorated markedly during the 1920s, even after correcting for the fact that a larger share of early issues were paid off by the time the defaults began. In addition, relatively small percentages of the bonds floated by some investment bankers were in default in 1937 regardless of when they were issued, while the majority of the issues of other underwriters were in default whether they were issued early or late in the 1920s. This result is essentially unaffected by the choice of 1937 as reference date. See Ilse Mintz, *Deterioration in the Quality of Foreign Bonds Issued in the United States, 1920–1930* (National Bureau of Economic Research, 1951), pp. 29–49, 54–58.

of excluding borrowers from new issues.[5] Although governments sometimes helped resolve defaults, military force was rarely used to safeguard
bondholders' interests.[6] More often, the governments of private creditors did not interfere, except to prevent discrimination by the debtor in
favor of creditors from another country.[7]

Several important differences exist between the prewar and postwar
lending arrangements for Eastern European and developing-country
borrowers. Most important, short- and medium-term bank lending at
floating interest rates has largely replaced fixed-rate bond financing. In
addition, banks' lending spreads (the margin above their cost of funds)
have typically been far below the risk premiums previously demanded
by bondholders. This in turn reflects how banks now respond to debt-
servicing problems. Instead of agreeing to partial debt relief, as they
used to, they stretch out debt repayments on market terms and thereby
avoid having to book losses on their loan portfolios. The ability of banks
to negotiate collectively with borrowers has made such rescheduling
much easier. The IMF's third-party role in renegotiations is also a major
departure from previous institutional arrangements.

Finally, the consequences of serious debt-servicing interruptions have
become more global since World War II because of changes in the
creditor-borrower relationship. First, the credit standings of all public-

5. Bondholders were occasionally quite aggressive in pursuing their claims. For
example, between 1879 and 1891 French bondholders, pressing for the payment of an 1832
issue, used wall posters, press advertisements, and sandwich boards to impede the sale of
new Portuguese issues. After these tactics contributed to the failure of an 1890 issue, a
settlement was reached in 1891. See William H. Wynne, *State Insolvency and Foreign
Bondholders*, vol. 2: *Case Histories* (Yale University Press, 1951), p. 363.
6. According to Edwin Borchard, "it cannot be said that military action in support of
bondholders is now or ever was an important phase of international relations." See
Borchard, *State Insolvency and Foreign Bondholders*, vol. 1: *General Principles* (Yale
University Press, 1951), p. 269.
7. Several of the interventions were quite spectacular. Two extreme cases of military
intervention involved a complete loss of sovereignty for the borrower country: the British
administration of Egypt from 1882 to 1907 and the French installation of Maximilian as
emperor of Mexico in 1863. Other famous cases included U.S. military action throughout
Central America and the Caribbean in the early 1900s and the blockade of Venezuela by
Great Britain, Germany, and Italy for two months in 1902 and 1903. When military force
was used, however, it was usually to achieve broader political objectives. For example,
U.S. military administration of customs houses was often used to prevent European
governments from expanding their presence in the Western hemisphere; the British
administration of Egypt was designed to protect the Suez Canal and Britain's far-ranging
empire; and the Venezuelan case involved many private and government claims for loss
of life and property (including the seizure of British ships) during the revolutions between
1898 and 1902. For details, see ibid., pp. 269–71, and Wynne, *State Insolvency and Foreign
Bondholders*, pp. 5–30, 577–616.

sector borrowers within the same country are now linked.[8] This is a result of central government guarantees on foreign debt and cross-default clauses that have been introduced in loan agreements. (Under cross-default clauses a country may be considered in default on all its loan agreements if it defaults on any one of them.) Second, the dependence of *country borrowers* on the renewal of short-term bank credits has introduced a new source of instability by making the international lending system vulnerable to credit withdrawals, from both countries and geographic regions, when confidence is shaken.[9] Third, the involvement of banks in foreign lending has created direct links between domestic banking systems and country borrowers that could affect Western economies profoundly if defaults were to occur.

Consequences of the Present Crisis

It is because of such global economic interdependence that the current debt crisis so seriously threatens the stability of the world economic order. For a creditor nation such as the United States, this threat has two dimensions. First, many U.S. domestic banks have large amounts of loans outstanding to distressed country borrowers, particularly in Latin America. Second, if current financial strains should lead to a sharp contraction in world trade, a sustained U.S. economic recovery would not be assured.[10] Apart from economic repercussions, failure to resolve the debt problem in an orderly way could also have far-reaching political

8. The status of individual borrowers today is not comparable with that of individual U.S. borrowers in the nineteenth century. U.S. debts were then contracted by a variety of state and private-sector entities with independently controlled sources of revenues and without cross-default guarantees. A state or railroad could, therefore, default without cutting off credit to the entire country.

9. The term *country borrower* in this study includes external borrowing by all entities within a particular country, regardless of whether they are publicly or privately owned.

10. The developing countries, which have become important trading partners of the West, absorbed 26 percent of merchandise exports from countries in the Organization for Economic Cooperation and Development in 1981. The United States is even more dependent on the developing countries for its exports: 38 percent of U.S. exports went to developing countries in 1981, of which nearly 17 percent went to Latin America. (See Rimmer de Vries, "Global Debt," statement prepared for the Subcommittee on International Economic Policy of the Senate Foreign Relations Committee, January 19, 1983, p. 17.) Mexico provides a good example of the speed with which contractions in the funding available to developing countries can affect trade flows. Its imports from the United States fell 58.9 percent in the fourth quarter of 1982 compared with the same period in 1981. See U.S. Department of Commerce, Bureau of Economic Analysis, *Survey of Current Business*, various issues (December 1982, March 1983), table S-17.

consequences in the third world and elsewhere. In particular, developing countries might consider establishing a debtors' cartel, leading to a direct confrontation between debtor and creditor nations.

This paper, in examining the policy implications of the global debt problem, focuses on two sets of issues. First, the current emergency lending system needs to be strengthened. Second, international bank lending must be reassessed to identify longer-term reforms that would reduce the likelihood of emergencies arising in the future. Such initiatives, however, must be accompanied by determined efforts to ensure an early global economic recovery.

A Statistical Analysis of International Bank Lending

The events most closely connected—at least chronologically—with the sharp increase in bank debt are the massive oil price increases of 1973–74 and 1979–80 and the worldwide recession of 1981–82. Table 1 shows the balance-of-payments position of the major groups of countries from 1973 to 1982. The pattern in 1973 is typical of that prevailing before the oil shocks: surpluses in the industrial countries were offset by deficits

Table 1. *Payments Balances on Current Account, 1973–82*[a]

Billions of dollars

| Year | Industrial countries | | Developing countries | | |
	Seven largest[b]	Other	Oil-exporting	Non-oil	Total[c]
1973	12.7	5.0	6.7	−11.6	12.8
1974	−4.9	−8.9	68.3	−37.0	17.4
1975	22.1	−4.3	35.4	−46.5	6.7
1976	7.5	−9.7	40.3	−32.0	6.1
1977	7.6	−12.6	30.8	−28.3	−2.4
1978	33.9	−3.5	2.9	−39.2	−5.8
1979	2.7	−12.9	69.8	−58.9	0.7
1980	−17.5	−26.2	116.4	−86.2	−13.7
1981	13.0	−16.7	68.6	−99.0	−34.1
1982[d]	23.5	−12.5	25.0	−97.0	−61.0

Source: International Monetary Fund, *Annual Report 1982*, p. 18.
a. On goods, services, and private transfers.
b. United States, Canada, Japan, West Germany, France, United Kingdom, and Italy.
c. Reflects errors, omissions, asymmetries in statistics, plus balance of listed groups with other countries (mainly the Soviet Union and Eastern European countries not in the IMF).
d. IMF projection, August 1982.

5

Table 2. *Current Account Financing of Non-Oil Developing Countries, 1973–81*
Billions of dollars

Item	1973	1974	1975	1976	1977	1978	1979	1980	1981
Current account deficit[a]	11.6	37.0	46.5	32.0	28.3	39.2	58.9	86.2	99.0
Financing through transactions not affecting net debt positions	10.1	13.0	11.8	12.0	14.9	17.2	23.0	24.1	26.3
Net unrequited transfers	5.4	6.9	7.1	7.4	8.3	8.2	10.9	12.3	12.9
Net direct investment flows	4.3	5.3	5.3	4.7	5.3	6.9	9.2	10.0	13.6
Net borrowing and use of reserves	1.5	23.9	34.7	20.1	13.4	22.0	35.9	62.1	72.7
Reduction of reserve assets[b]	-9.7	-2.4	1.9	-13.8	-12.4	-15.8	-12.4	-4.9	-1.6
Net external borrowing	11.2	23.3	32.9	31.2	25.8	37.8	48.4	67.1	74.3

Source: IMF, *Annual Report 1982*, p. 34.
a. Balance on goods, services, and private transfers.
b. A minus sign indicates an accumulation of reserves.

in the non-oil developing countries, with the oil exporters near balance.[11] The first oil shock changed this pattern radically. In 1974 the industrial countries had small deficits, the non-oil developing countries had large deficits, and oil exporters enjoyed huge surpluses. From 1975 to 1978 the surpluses of members of the Organization of Petroleum Exporting Countries (OPEC) gradually vanished, as surpluses reappeared in the larger industrial countries.

The second oil shock led to almost the same balance-of-payments pattern. The OPEC nations ran huge surpluses in 1979 and 1980, but these disappeared almost as quickly as they came. Among oil-consuming nations, the balance-of-payments position of the larger industrial countries shifted most dramatically, but they restored their traditional surpluses by 1981. In that year smaller industrial countries were moving slowly toward balance, but the non-oil developing countries were mired in large deficits. These divergent trends in balance-of-payments positions became more pronounced in 1981 and 1982 because of the continuing recession in the West.[12]

Of course, deficits do not necessarily imply an increase in bank lending to developing nations; other possible sources of current account financing include direct investment, foreign-aid grants, and the running down of reserves. However, debt has become the main source of financing in recent years (table 2). In 1973, before the first oil shock, nondebt sources financed five-sixths of the deficits of developing countries and most borrowings were used to build up reserves. From 1974 to 1979, however, nondebt sources provided only one-third to one-half of the much larger volume of financing, and since then this ratio has fallen even further. In addition, while debt has become a primary source of financing, the extent to which that debt has been offset by increases in reserves has diminished rapidly: the ratio of reserves accumulation to net external borrowings

11. Oil-exporting countries, as defined by the IMF, are those developing countries whose oil exports account for at least two-thirds of the country's total exports and whose oil exports equal at least 100 million barrels a year (roughly equal to 1 percent of annual world oil exports). This definition is based on 1977–79 averages. All other developing countries are defined as non-oil developing countries.

12. The last column of table 1 shows a negative world current account balance that far exceeds the probable balance of IMF members with the Soviet Union and Eastern Europe. Two important causes of that discrepancy are the underreporting of transportation services earnings by "flags-of-convenience" nations and the underreporting of foreign investment income, especially by OECD and OPEC states. For further details on this problem, see Organization for Economic Cooperation and Development, "The World Current Account Discrepancy," *Occasional Studies*, supplement to the *OECD Economic Outlook* (Paris: OECD, June 1982), pp. 46–63.

7

Table 3. *Disbursed Debt of Non-OPEC Developing Countries, Selected Years, 1971–82*

Billions of dollars

Type of financing	1971	1975	1977	1980	1981[a]	1982[b]
Medium- and long-term debt	75	152	227	385	445	520
DAC countries and capital markets[c]	58	115	170	291	332	386
Official development assistance	21	30	36	49	49	55
Total export credits	20	30	45	80	91	105
Export credits from banks	n.a.	n.a.	13	33	39	49
Capital markets[d]	17	54	89	162	192	228
Bank loans	10	43	69	132	156	182
Multilateral organizations	10	20	30	52	60	70
Concessional loans	6	9	13	23	27	31
Other sources[e]	7	18	26	42	53	64
Short-term bank debt	n.a.	n.a.	37	89	110	134

Source: Organization for Economic Cooperation and Development, *External Debt of Developing Countries: 1982 Survey* (Paris: OECD, 1982), pp. 28, 43.

n.a. Not available.

a. Preliminary.

b. Estimated.

c. The Development Assistance Committee (DAC) members are Australia, Austria, Belgium, Canada, Denmark, Finland, France, Italy, Japan, the Netherlands, New Zealand, Norway, Sweden, Switzerland, the United Kingdom, the United States, and West Germany.

d. Bank loans (other than export credits), bonds, and other private lending.

e. Council for Mutual Economic Assistance (CMEA) countries (the Soviet Union, Eastern Europe, Cuba, and Vietnam) and OPEC and other developing countries.

averaged 45 percent from 1976 to 1978, fell to 25 percent in 1979, and plunged below 8 percent in both 1980 and 1981.

While developing countries have begun relying more on loans to finance current account deficits, commercial banks have been providing an increasing share of those loans. Bank loans (excluding export credits) were the source of only 13 percent of the total medium- and long-term debt outstanding in 1971, while concessional loans accounted for over one-third and export credits for one-quarter of the outstanding debt that year (table 3). By the end of 1982, however, bank loans were the single largest source of medium- and long-term funds for developing countries, providing 35 percent of their financing. Concessional loans and export credits accounted for only 16.5 percent and 20.2 percent, respectively, of their financing. Furthermore, the share of total bank credits (including export credits) in medium- and long-term debt rose from 36.1 percent in 1977 (the first year for which such calculations are possible) to 44.4 percent in 1982. During this same period the amount of short-term bank loans grew much faster than other forms of bank debt and medium- and long-term debt.

Before examining the buildup of bank debt more closely, it is useful to note the division of developing countries' external assets and liabilities between obligations with fixed and those with floating interest rates (table 4). Among countries not in OPEC or the Organization for Economic Cooperation and Development (OECD), short-term assets and liabilities were roughly equal from 1980 to 1982, although the net short-term position has deteriorated slightly. On the medium- and long-term account, however, floating-rate liabilities far exceed floating-rate assets for these countries. Assuming that the interest rates on short-term assets and liabilities move parallel to market interest rates, the value of floating-rate debt for these countries changed from a net debt of $90 billion in 1980 to a net debt of $166 billion in 1982. Net interest payments in these countries were, therefore, quickly affected by changes in interest rates. This was especially true for the four largest non-OPEC borrowers (Argentina, Brazil, Mexico, and South Korea), whose net floating-rate debt increased from $79 billion in 1980 to $140 billion in 1982.

Table 5 shows the recent buildup in bank debt. In 1977 Eastern European nations accounted for over $40 billion in loans, and all developing-country borrowers for $127.7 billion. The Eastern European debt increased to $71.4 billion in 1981 before declining to $63.9 billion in mid-1982 and $63.1 billion at the end of 1982. The recent decrease was due partly to the weakness of the German mark—the currency in which a large part of Eastern European debt is denominated—and partly to the difficulties of such countries as Poland and Yugoslavia in raising new funds.[13]

The debts of developing countries increased even more rapidly. Bank loans outstanding reached $343.5 billion by June 1982, before the crisis finally slowed the growth by immobilizing the normal functioning of the market. Yet loans to developing countries still reached $362.7 billion by the end of 1982. Argentina, Brazil, Chile, Mexico, the Philippines, South Korea, and Venezuela accounted for most of this bank debt. Their share, which was at its lowest in 1978 at 51.5 percent, increased continuously to 62.7 percent in June 1982 and then fell to 61.7 percent during the next six months. Mexico and Brazil have the largest bank debts outstanding. Clearly banks have concentrated their lending in a small group of

13. At least in the case of Poland, the reduction in bank debt was also due in part to the transfer of U.S. bank credits guaranteed by the Commodity Credit Corporation (a part of the U.S. Department of Agriculture) back to the CCC when Poland did not make its payments on time. For details, see Edward Cowan, "U.S. to Pay Part of Polish Debt; Default Avoided," *New York Times*, February 1, 1982.

9

Table 4. *Estimated External Assets and Liabilities of Non-OPEC, Non-OECD Developing Countries, 1980–82*[a]
Billions of dollars

Type of liability and asset	Liabilities			Assets			Balance[b]		
	1980	1981	1982	1980	1981	1982	1980	1981	1982
Medium- and long-term	322	372	438	25	32	40	-297	-340	-398
Fixed interest rates	216	240	272	22	27	33	-194	-213	-239
Floating interest rates	106	132	166	3	5	7	-103	-127	-159
Short-term[c]	93	103	121	106	110	114	13	7	-7
Total	415	475	559	131	142	154	-284	-333	-405
Fixed interest rates	216	240	272	22	27	33	-194	-213	-239
Floating interest rates[c]	199	235	287	109	115	121	-90	-120	-166
Argentina, Brazil, Mexico, and South Korea	111	141	173	32	31	33	-79	-110	-140

Source: OECD, *External Debt of Developing Countries: 1982 Survey*, p. 32.
a. Excluding direct investment, gold, and IMF transactions.
b. A negative sign indicates that liabilities exceed assets.
c. All short-term instruments are treated as floating-rate instruments.

Table 5. *Bank Loans Outstanding to Eastern Europe and Developing Countries, 1977–82*[a]

Billions of dollars unless otherwise specified

Country or group of countries	December 1977	December 1978	December 1979	December 1980	December 1981	June 1982	December 1982
Eastern Europe[b]	40.2	53.7	64.4	70.1	71.4	63.9	63.1
Developing countries	127.7	174.2	235.6	279.6	326.7	343.5	362.7
Seven major developing-country borrowers	69.5	89.7	128.0	165.8	201.2	215.4	223.9
Argentina	4.9	6.7	13.4	19.9	24.8	25.3	25.7
Brazil	25.0	31.7	38.6	45.7	52.5	55.3	60.5
Chile	1.6	2.9	4.9	7.3	10.5	11.8	11.6
Mexico	20.3	23.3	30.9	42.5	57.1	64.4	62.9
Philippines	3.4	4.2	7.4	9.3	10.2	11.4	12.6
South Korea	5.2	6.9	12.0	16.7	19.9	20.0	23.2
Venezuela	9.1	14.0	20.8	24.3	26.2	27.2	27.5
Addenda							
Proportion of all developing-country borrowing (percent)							
Seven major countries	54.4	51.5	54.3	59.3	61.6	62.7	61.7
Brazil	19.6	18.2	16.4	16.3	16.1	16.1	16.7
Mexico	15.9	13.3	13.1	15.2	17.5	18.7	17.3

Source: Bank for International Settlements (BIS), *Maturity Distribution of International Bank Lending,* various issues.

a. These figures give the aggregate external positions of banks in Austria, Belgium-Luxembourg, Canada, Denmark, France, Ireland, Italy, Japan, the Netherlands, Sweden, Switzerland, the United Kingdom, the United States, and West Germany and of a number of their affiliates in other countries. The figures for banks with head offices in the United States are consolidated to include the positions of all their foreign affiliates. For banks with head offices in other reporting countries, the figures include the positions of affiliates in the major offshore banking centers.

b. Including Yugoslavia.

countries, despite the fact that Western banks hold claims on public- or private-sector borrowers from over 120 developing countries in Asia, Africa, Latin America, and the Caribbean.

The short average maturity of this debt has been an important factor in the current problems. Although the proportion of short-term debt has increased only slightly since 1977 (table 6), the pressure this places on borrowers has increased considerably because of the rapid growth in the volume of short-term lending. For example, the volume of bank loans to developing countries due within one year totaled over $170 billion in June 1982 and thus exceeded the value of all bank loans outstanding to these countries in 1977. Furthermore, the decline in the share of short-term debt in the second half of 1982 probably reflects bank decisions not to roll over short-term loans as they matured, rather than a strategic decision by borrowers to use longer-term debt. Short-term loans to Mexico in particular increased sharply, from $8.3 billion in 1977 to some $32 billion in mid-1982. This exacerbated Mexico's funding problems

Table 6. *Maturity Distribution of Bank Lending to Developing Countries, 1977–82*

Borrower	Loans outstanding (billions of dollars)	Maturity distribution (percent)			
		Up to one year	Other short-term[a]	Medium-term[b]	Unallo-cated
All developing countries					
December 1977	127.7	48.1	11.1	39.6	1.3
December 1979	235.6	46.3	8.1	36.8	8.7
December 1981	326.7	49.8	7.3	35.2	7.7
June 1982	343.5	50.0	7.3	35.4	7.3
December 1982	362.7	49.5	6.1	36.1	8.3
Brazil					
December 1977	25.0	31.5	12.7	54.5	1.3
December 1979	38.6	29.2	10.3	52.1	8.4
December 1981	52.5	34.7	8.1	47.5	9.6
June 1982	55.3	33.7	7.7	48.6	9.9
December 1982	60.5	34.9	5.7	49.6	9.8
Mexico					
December 1977	20.3	41.0	13.5	44.6	1.0
December 1979	30.9	34.5	10.8	48.6	6.0
December 1981	57.1	48.7	8.3	39.7	3.3
June 1982	64.4	50.0	8.8	38.2	3.0
December 1982	62.9	47.6	7.1	41.4	3.9

Source: BIS, *Maturity Distribution of International Bank Lending,* various issues. Figures are rounded.
a. Between one and two years.
b. Over two years.

during 1982 and helped precipitate its default. Brazil controlled the situation somewhat better, with a short-term debt of just under $19 billion by mid-1982. Yet this amount was more than enough to force Brazil into rescheduling when Mexico's default led to doubts about the ability of other Latin American borrowers to meet their obligations. Even without Mexico's difficulties, Brazil's continuous need to roll over its large short-term debt could eventually have led to serious problems.

Measures of the debt-service burden also show how the maturity distribution of the debt has made the overall debt problem worse. Debt service, calculated as the ratio of interest payments plus amortization of medium- and long-term debt to exports of goods and services,[14] rose from 20 percent in 1980 to 28 percent in 1982 for the developing countries not in OPEC.[15] This increase itself may have caused some banks to

14. Exports are perhaps the most common proxy for a country's ability to service its debt.

15. "Statement of Paul A. Volcker, chairman of the Board of Governors of the Federal Reserve System, to the Committee on Banking, Finance and Urban Affairs of the House of Representatives," February 2, 1983, table 1.

reevaluate their lending. The potential short-term pressures on a country, however, are better measured by the total debt-service burden, calculated as interest payments on gross debt, amortization of medium- and long-term debt, and repayments of short-term debt, because this figure includes the large component of short-term debt. On this basis it has been estimated that debt service in 1983 will exceed 100 percent of exports for each of the five major Latin American borrowers and will reach 154 percent for Argentina. Even if short-term claims account for most of these percentages, countries with total debt-service ratios of this magnitude are clearly vulnerable to funding crises. These estimates may also help to explain why Asian borrowers have escaped funding problems so far: South Korea and the Philippines, for example, have estimated debt-service ratios of 49 percent and 79 percent, respectively.[16] These countries, therefore, can more easily cope with a shortfall of funds by limiting imports.

Table 7 shows the U.S. share of bank loans to the seven major developing-country borrowers. U.S. banks accounted for 39.2 percent of all bank loans to these countries as of June 1982. The share of U.S. banks in loans to non-OPEC developing countries, however, has declined sharply in recent years, from almost 50 percent in 1977 to just under 37 percent in 1982.[17] U.S. banks have been much less active in Eastern Europe. The largest U.S. exposure in that region is $2.5 billion to Yugoslavia.

U.S. banks have not participated equally in lending to developing countries. As of June 1982 U.S. banks had $98.6 billion in loans outstanding to non-OPEC developing countries, or 148.9 percent of the banks' total capital (table 8).[18] The nine largest banks had extended slightly over three-fifths of these loans and were heavily committed in terms of other measures: their outstanding loans amounted to 10.6 percent of their assets and 222.5 percent of their capital. Still, it is clear that other American banks have also been involved in foreign lending, as even the smaller banks—that is, all but the twenty-four largest institutions—have $19.3 billion in claims outstanding to non-OPEC developing countries. Furthermore, banks have concentrated their lend-

16. De Vries, "Global Debt."
17. "Statement of Paul A. Volcker," table 2.
18. These figures understate the maximum risk the debt crisis poses to U.S. banks for three reasons. First, the definition of capital is broad; it includes equity and subordinated debt. Second, borrowers from OPEC nations are excluded, even though they account for more than 20 percent of Western lending. Third, Eastern European borrowers are not included; if they were, these figures might increase by 10 percent.

Table 7. *U.S. and Non-U.S. Bank Claims on Major Developing-Country Borrowers, June 1982*

Billions of dollars unless otherwise specified

Country	Total bank debt	Owed to U.S. banks	Owed to non-U.S. banks	U.S. share (percent)
Mexico	64.4	24.3	40.1	37.7
Brazil	55.3	20.7	34.6	37.4
Venezuela	27.2	11.1	16.1	40.8
South Korea	20.0	8.7	11.3	43.5
Argentina	25.3	8.6	16.7	34.0
Chile	11.8	6.3	5.5	53.4
Philippines	11.4	4.8	6.6	42.1

Source: "Statement of Paul A. Volcker, chairman of the Board of Governors of the Federal Reserve System, to the Committee on Banking, Finance and Urban Affairs of the House of Representatives," February 2, 1983, table 3.

Table 8. *Claims on Non-OPEC Developing Countries Held by U.S. Banks, June 1982*

Item	Total (billions of dollars)	Share of total assets (percent)	Share of total capital (percent)
Claims on non-OPEC developing countries held by:			
All reporting banks	98.6	8.3	148.9
Nine largest banks	60.3	10.6	222.5
Next fifteen largest banks	19.0	7.9	149.6
All other reporting banks	19.3	5.0	73.1
Claims on Argentina, Brazil, and Mexico held by:			
All reporting banks	52.4	4.4	83.6
Nine largest banks	30.5	5.4	112.5
Next fifteen largest banks	10.3	4.3	81.1
All other reporting banks	11.6	3.0	43.9

Source: "Statement of Paul A. Volcker," tables 4 and 5.

ing in Latin America, with three countries—Mexico, Brazil, and Argentina—receiving over half the loans to non-OPEC developing countries granted by each group of banks. The range of banks involved in foreign lending and their large commitments to developing countries—particularly in Latin America—are evidence that the consequences of the withdrawal of regional banks from international lending would be serious.[19]

The Relationship between Banks and Country Borrowers

A variety of economic, legal, and political circumstances have influenced the relationships between banks and country borrowers over the last decade. For banks, lending to governments and companies in Eastern European and developing countries was a natural extension of movements already taking place in international financial markets. Banks had begun to follow their domestic customers overseas after World War II, and by the time of the first oil shock they had become active in syndicated lending to multinational corporations and Western governments. In addition, some banks wanted to forge new long-term relationships with non-Western borrowers. Others—particularly smaller banks—were willing to venture overseas, at least temporarily, because of reduced credit demands and fierce competition in their traditional domestic markets. Another impetus to expand was changes taking place in the market's structure. One was the development of Eurocurrency deposits—that is, funds deposited with a bank office outside the currency's country of origin—which expanded the range of funding sources available to banks. Another change was the use of margins over the London Interbank Offered Rate (LIBOR) in the pricing of loans, which reduced some of the interest-rate risk involved in the use of short-term deposits to fund medium-term loans. Other important structural developments were cross-default clauses in loan agreements, which placed all bank claims on an equal footing, and the syndication of credits, in which one or several large banks organize loans and sell most of the credit to other banks. Syndication lowered the information and management costs for entities that needed to borrow large amounts.

Country borrowers pursue foreign loans for several reasons. First, such loans allow both companies and governments to finance investments that will increase income or exports. Second, foreign loans offer countries flexibility in their attempts to smooth the adjustment to

---

19. For example, if the nine largest banks had to replace the small banks as lenders to non-OPEC developing countries, the exposure of the large banks would climb to $79.6 billion, equal to 293.7 percent of capital, while their exposure to Argentina, Brazil, and Mexico would climb to $42.1 billion and 155.4 percent of capital.

permanent or temporary changes in economic conditions.[20] Finally, governments may borrow for political reasons, such as to retain or consolidate power.[21] In all these cases they can borrow against the capacity to pay out of future income and exports.

Bank lending must also be considered in light of the maturity mismatching inherent in such lending. Although banking has always involved some maturity transformation, with the average maturity of bank assets (loans) exceeding the average maturity of bank liabilities (deposits), banks have pursued predominantly short-term investments because of the potential draw-down of the deposits that fund their activities. Many of the transactions with country borrowers, however, were designed to finance medium-term adjustment or long-term investment projects. Banks overcame this obstacle in part through the use of medium-term floating-rate loans, which removed the lenders' interest-rate risk. Borrowers, on the other hand, were unwilling to pay the higher interest rates the market required on long-term funds (such as bonds) and decided to use shorter-term bank loans to fund their long-term needs. The funding of long-term investments with shorter-term bank loans, however, entails several risks, especially the risk that banks might want to withdraw their loans before the borrower's investments come to fruition, regardless of the borrower's capacity to repay its debts. Borrowers have tended to assume that loans could be renewed automatically when they become due. The degree to which borrowers rely on short-term funds further increases the risks of maturity mismatching.

20. In particular, a country facing a temporary worsening of its prospects (perhaps because of a drop in export income or oil expenditures) should dissave initially, to adjust the time pattern of consumption with the least loss of welfare. This shows up as a temporary current account deficit. A country adjusting to a permanent worsening of economic conditions may dissave initially to reduce adjustment costs but eventually must cut its consumption. Thus, while a country's current account deficit may worsen at first, the eventual decline in consumption should lead to smaller current account deficits. Conversely, a country facing permanently improved prospects should be able to borrow against the future. This would be particularly true if it needs investment to realize those improvements. For a detailed discussion of these propositions, see Jeffrey D. Sachs, "The Current Account and Macroeconomic Adjustment in the 1970s," *Brookings Papers on Economic Activity, 1:1981*, pp. 215–25 (hereafter *BPEA*); and Maurice Obstfeld, "Transitory Terms-of-Trade Shocks and the Current Account: The Case of Constant Time Preference," International Finance Discussion Paper 194 (Washington, D.C.: Board of Governors of the Federal Reserve System, 1981).

21. At least one study has tried to analyze the extent to which countries used their loans for adjustment and political purposes. See Benjamin J. Cohen, in collaboration with Fabio Basagni, *Banks and the Balance of Payments: Private Lending in the International Adjustment Process* (Montclair, N.J.: Allanheld, Osmun, 1981).

The Effect of Economic Events since 1973 on International Lending

The Eastern European and developing countries started the 1970s with a low level of bank and nonbank debt. Given the changes in the structure of the international banking market, in economic conditions, and in the attitudes of banks and borrowers toward lending, it was natural for a certain amount of borrowing to occur; or, as one central banker remarked, there was a "vacuum to be filled."[22]

The oil shock of 1973–74 had a significant effect on international lending. At first there was considerable uncertainty about its effect on the long-term prospects of non-OPEC developing countries in relation to the industrial nations. Clearly, however, borrowing was necessary to smooth the adjustment to the oil shock. Besides other nonbank funding sources, a special oil facility was set up at the IMF to make such financing easier. Still, commercial loans quickly became the main source of funds for a small group of borrowers—the newly industrializing countries.[23] The continued availability of such funds appeared likely, since the oil shock seemed to have improved these countries' prospects in relation to the prospects of the developed world, at least to the extent that the newly industrializing countries continued to grow rapidly, while the West fell into its deepest postwar slump. Real growth rates in most of these countries were impressive, the volume of exports increased rapidly, and domestic investment (measured by the ratio of gross fixed capital formation to gross domestic absorption) increased after 1973.[24] Thus the first oil shock, by illustrating the ability of the newly industrializing countries to compete in world markets, also seemed to show that large-scale international lending was viable.[25]

After the second oil shock of 1979–80 the debt picture began to worsen. The global economic system was subjected to a number of strains (some temporary, some long lasting), which contributed to the eventual breakdown in international lending. The second oil shock

22. Henry C. Wallich, "Financing Developing Countries," speech delivered at the Annual Conference for U.S. Commercial Bankers, February 18, 1983, p. 2.

23. These countries include six of the seven largest borrowers; the other large borrower, Venezuela—an oil exporter—also experienced improved prospects through the rise in oil prices.

24. Robert Solomon, "The Debt of Developing Countries: Another Look," *BPEA*, *2:1981*, pp. 601–02.

25. Interest rates adjusted for inflation, or real interest rates, were barely positive and perhaps even negative, making loans even more attractive to borrowers.

emphasized the continued need for further real adjustment by the major developing-country and Eastern European borrowers. It was also becoming apparent that the favorable performance of developing nations in the mid-1970s had resulted in part from the availability of bank financing. Although it might have been appropriate after the second oil shock for developing countries to borrow funds on a temporary basis to finance the needed adjustments, a permanent expansion of debt was not called for. Even if countries' debt capacity had been unaffected by the rise in oil prices, there was little room left for further borrowing against that capacity.

At the same time, the cost of financing had also increased considerably. This resulted less from an increase in the spreads borrowers had to pay than from a sharp rise in the base cost of funds. Although the real interest rate banks paid for Eurodollar deposits was slightly negative in the mid-1970s, the real interest rate varied between 4 and 8 percent in the early 1980s.[26] Furthermore, since the real rate on Eurodollar deposits has averaged between 2 and 3 percent historically, it would be unwise to assume that real interest rates will return to zero.[27] With December 1982 levels of bank debt as a base, a real interest rate of 3 percent would cost developing countries about $10.9 billion (1982 dollars) a year.

Finally, a third negative factor had entered the picture by the early 1980s. The 1980–82 global recession reduced both the volumes and prices of exports for developing-country borrowers. Although this was a temporary setback, it forced those countries to increase their debts when lenders were revising downward their estimates of the debtors' prospects.

All these factors were unfavorable for the borrowing countries and

26. From 1975 to 1978 the interest rate on three-month Eurodollar deposits averaged 6.86 percent, while inflation, as measured by the change in the GNP price deflator for the United States, averaged 6.91 percent, implying a real interest rate on Eurodollar deposits of minus 0.05 percent. This same measure of the real interest rate averaged 4.69 percent, 7.35 percent, and 7.13 percent in 1980, 1981, and 1982, respectively. The GNP price deflator data are available in *Economic Report of the President*, February 1983, p. 166. Interest rate data are from several publications of the Board of Governors of the Federal Reserve System. Data for 1964 to 1970 are available in *Banking and Monetary Statistics, 1941–1970* (The Board, 1976), p. 676; for 1971 to 1979, in *Annual Statistical Digest, 1970–1979* (The Board, 1981), p. 162; and for 1980 to 1982, in *Federal Reserve Bulletin*, vol. 69 (March 1983), p. A28.

27. Data on Eurodollar deposits rates have been available only since 1964. From 1964 to 1980 the three-month Eurodollar deposit rate averaged 7.71 percent, while inflation, as measured by the GNP price deflator, averaged 5.55 percent, implying a real rate of 2.16 percent. Data from 1964 to 1982 give a real rate on Eurodollar deposits of 2.71 percent. Ibid.

led to increases in debt that eventually proved unsustainable. Although it may be argued that the market breakdown in 1982 resulted mainly from a rare constellation of unfavorable events, that interpretation does not adequately explain the market's response to the deteriorating global economic climate in 1980–82. After all, until early 1982 bank credit to developing countries continued to increase rapidly, with only a moderate upturn in lending spreads (risk premiums). This suggests that neither lenders nor borrowers were adjusting to the changed economic environment. Then, in the wake of the Falkland Islands crisis and Mexico's difficulties, there was a sudden contraction in lending that quickly transformed a handful of debt-servicing problems into a generalized debt crisis. Therefore a full explanation of the events of 1982 must also take into account the unique characteristics of international lending.

The Nature of Country Risk

The key differences between domestic and international lending can be summed up in the single phrase "country risk."[28] This has been defined as "the possibility that sovereign borrowers of a particular country may be unable or unwilling, and other borrowers unable, to fulfill their foreign obligations for reasons beyond the usual risks which arise in relation to all lending."[29] The concept of country risk encompasses many situations. For example, there may be no legal redress against a sovereign borrower that reneges on its external obligations, a situation known as sovereign risk. Another possible scenario is transfer risk, in which private-sector borrowers, though subject to legal process, may be unable to obtain the necessary foreign exchange to service their foreign debt.

It would seem that sovereign credits, which borrowers may be either unable or unwilling to repay, are more risky than private-sector credits, in which the only danger is the borrower's inability to repay. However, recent events suggest that when a country is unable to meet its external obligations as they fall due, the private sector tends to be last in line for scarce foreign exchange or is somehow placed at a disadvantage in relation to public-sector borrowers. In Mexico, for example, private

28. Some of the arguments presented in this section appeared in Richard S. Dale, "Country Risk and Bank Regulation," *The Banker*, March 1983, pp. 41–48.

29. Group of Thirty, *Risks in International Bank Lending* (New York: Group of Thirty, 1982), p. 6.

companies (often U.S. multinationals) with loans in hard currencies have had trouble getting foreign exchange on any terms,[30] while in Argentina the authorities have in effect unilaterally converted short-term corporate debt into medium-term public-sector debt.[31]

More generally, exchange-rate depreciation and other adjustments that may ultimately ease a country's debt-servicing problems can considerably strain private-sector borrowers with hard currency liabilities. A sudden shift to higher local currency interest rates, such as may be prescribed as part of an adjustment program, may further weaken the financial condition of corporate borrowers. Paradoxically, therefore, measures designed to relieve a debtor country's problems may reduce the credit standing of private borrowers within that country.

Interbank lending may also involve country risk, regardless of whether the debtor bank is state or privately owned. Funds placed with the foreign branch of another bank are subject to transfer risk arising within both the country in which the branch is situated and the country of the branch's parent. Moreover, the foreign offices of a bank with head offices in a debtor country may have extensive foreign-currency claims on its home country. Finally, the parent bank's central bank may not be in a position to act as lender of last resort in foreign currency if it is faced with a national foreign-exchange crisis. For all these reasons, the offices of a bank with headquarters in a problem country can succumb to funding difficulties in its international operations.[32] Interbank claims, therefore, are exposed to country risk arising from developments in the borrowing bank's country of origin.

Central to the concept of country risk is the fact that legal recourse against a defaulting government offers little protection to the lender. A legal suit in the courts of the borrowing country may not be entertained or, if it is, may not be successful or result in an enforceable judgment. On the other hand, redress in the courts of the lender's country may not be possible if sovereign immunity is invoked and cannot be effective if

30. For the arrangements eventually agreed on for the rescheduling of Mexico's private-sector debt, see "Banks Agree to Mexico's Debt Plan," *Financial Times* (London), April 7, 1983.

31. In effect, the Argentine Central Bank refused to honor its foreign currency swap agreements with local companies that had borrowed funds from abroad. See James L. Rowe, Jr., "Argentine Bank Refuses to Pay Foreign Debt," *Washington Post*, November 20, 1982.

32. Brazilian banks had particularly severe problems in the dollar market in late 1982 and had to be supported several times. For details, see Andrew Whitley, "Brazil's Total Debt Over $100bn," *Financial Times*, December 13, 1982; and Whitley, "U.S. Banks Bail Out Banco do Brasil for Third Time," ibid., December 15, 1982.

there are no assets to seize. Although more complex considerations apply, legal redress may also be impossible when a private-sector borrower cannot meet its external obligations because it lacks access to foreign exchange.[33]

Without legal redress, country borrowers and bank lenders are bound together not by enforceable contractual relations but by implicit threats: the lenders' collective threat to exclude a defaulting borrower from international capital markets and the borrower's threat to default if new funding should be denied. The disciplinary mechanism is therefore based on sanctions, not remedies.

Nor are country borrowers subject to the legal conditions routinely applied in domestic markets. In the case of corporate borrowing, bond covenants are available to restrict the borrower from taking certain actions after the debt is incurred.[34] Such provisions, however, are unenforceable against countries and so are not included in international loan agreements. As a result lenders have little or no control over a country's prospective indebtedness.

Apart from the unusual legal characteristics of international lending, there are special problems involved in assessing the creditworthiness of foreign countries. It is a troublesome paradox, for example, that although countries cannot go bankrupt, they may still fail to pay their debts. In an attempt to assess the risk of failure to pay, some analysts have tried to draw a distinction, borrowed from domestic corporate finance, between solvency and liquidity problems. For instance, one recent study claims that a solvency problem arises when the real interest payment on marginal foreign borrowing exceeds the increase in national income made possible by such borrowing. A liquidity problem, on the other hand, means that the borrower is unable to obtain the foreign exchange with which to service its foreign debt on schedule—that is, there is a breakdown in the refunding mechanism.[35] The study concludes that when a country has borrowed so much abroad that its domestic income is adversely affected, because investment returns fall short of borrowing costs, the present value of external debt needs to be reduced by some form of debt relief.

33. Under Mexican law, for instance, a company can satisfy its contractual obligations to a foreign bank that has lent it dollars by placing the local currency equivalent, at a specified exchange rate, with the central bank. If Mexican law were applied, the foreign bank would then have no legal recourse against the company nor, apparently, against an external guarantor of that company's dollar debt.

34. These restrictions may concern dividend payments, debt ceilings, maintenance of assets, and disclosure requirements.

35. See Robert Z. Aliber, "A Conceptual Approach to the Analysis of External Debt of the Developing Countries," Working Paper 421 (Washington, D.C.: World Bank, 1980).

From an operational point of view, however, this distinction is not very useful. In particular, if it turns out that the funds borrowed have failed to augment the debtor country's national income, it seems unrealistic to expect the lender to forgo some portion of what is owed to him simply because the country is now defined as insolvent. Indeed, if the only security for banks' international loans were provided by the net proceeds from investments made possible by the loans, rather than by the country's general capacity to generate foreign exchange, banks would become equity investors, and their enthusiasm for such lending would presumably diminish.

There are other problems with trying to distinguish between a country's capacity to pay its debts and its willingness to do so. The only unambiguous indicator of a country's unwillingness to pay is outright debt repudiation. Between repudiation on the one hand and timely debt repayment on the other, there is a range of possible debt-servicing problems that may reflect varying degrees of both incapacity and unwillingness to repay debts. For instance, in the current spate of debt reschedulings, bank creditors usually commit themselves to providing a specified amount of new money as part of the rescheduling package. Since these funds are not obtainable from the market, lenders presumably are motivated by the implicit threat of the borrower's unilateral default. As the recent literature on default risk suggests, in such complex negotiating situations no clear line can be drawn between a borrower's capacity and willingness to meet its obligations.[36]

The creditworthiness of borrowers in a given country is thus not only a matter of credit risk in the traditional sense but also a political matter, determined by the interest and ability of the country's government to manage its economy so as to generate enough foreign exchange. Because of this political dimension, questions of solvency versus liquidity, or capacity to pay versus willingness to pay, are difficult to answer. Therefore the concept of country risk is necessarily a murky one.

The differences between corporate risk and country risk suggest that greater dangers may exist in international lending. One wonders, therefore, why banks are prepared to engage in large-scale lending to sovereign borrowers without collateral, with no control over the use to which funds are put, without foreknowledge of or control over the debtor's subsequent borrowing, and with no effective legal redress should default occur.

36. See, for instance, Jeffrey Sachs and Daniel Cohen, "LDC Borrowing with Default Risk," Working Paper 925 (National Bureau of Economic Research, July 1982).

One view has been that banks make these loans because they know they will be bailed out by their own governments. Indeed, in some cases banks probably have counted on official bailouts. But this explanation seems insufficient, because banks were not bailed out in the occasional reschedulings of the 1970s (the terms of the current reschedulings and suggested new regulations also have not offered a bailout). Instead, banks apparently rely on three kinds of safeguards: the self-interest of countries in honoring their external obligations; the risk-spreading protection offered by geographic diversification; and the ability to withdraw loans or at least reduce commitments before debt servicing is interrupted.

The growing literature on default risk explores when it might be to a country's advantage to discontinue servicing its external debt, on the assumption that creditors respond to unilateral default by excluding the borrower from future loans.[37] One conclusion that emerges from this literature is that it would be in the lenders' interest to assign to each borrowing country "a maximum safe level of debt such that the total benefits of default (which increase with debt) just equal the total costs of default."[38] Since there is currently no way to agree on or enforce such an aggregate credit ceiling, however, lenders can never be sure that borrowers will not pass the point at which default becomes a serious option. Furthermore, since countries as such do not borrow, but governments do, there is always a possibility of politically motivated borrowing calculated to prolong a particular regime's position in power. Governments may also engage in acts or threats of default that ignore the longer-term costs of exclusion from international financial markets. The self-interest of the borrowing country, therefore, is uncertain security.

The second source of security for banks is geographic diversification. The conventional view has been that the economic performance of borrowers in different countries is unrelated enough to spread risks effectively.[39] Recent events have shown, however, that certain elements

37. See, for example, Jonathan Eaton and Mark Gersovitz, "LDC Participation in International Financial Markets: Debt and Reserves," *Journal of Development Economics*, vol. 7 (March 1980), pp. 3–22; Eaton and Gersovitz, "Debt with Potential Repudiation: Theoretical and Empirical Analysis," *Review of Economic Studies*, vol. 48 (April 1981), pp. 289–310; Jeffrey Sachs, "LDC Debt in the 1980s: Risk and Reforms," Working Paper 861 (National Bureau of Economic Research, February 1982); and Sachs and Cohen, "LDC Borrowing with Default Risk."

38. Jonathan Eaton and Mark Gersovitz, "Poor-Country Borrowing in Private Financial Markets and the Repudiation Issue," Princeton Studies in International Finance 47 (Princeton University, Department of Economics, 1981), p. 13.

39. Laurie S. Goodman, "Bank Lending to Non-OPEC LDCs: Are Risks Diversifia-

of systematic or nondiversifiable risk in international lending have been underestimated. The role of common external shocks, such as high interest rates, global recession, and falling commodity prices, has been mentioned earlier. In addition, under disturbed financial conditions debt problems tend to spread from one country to another by way of contagious credit withdrawals, as illustrated by the effect of Mexico's financial troubles on the rest of Latin America. The reason for such contagion appears to be that the credit standing of a country in debt to a large number of lenders depends not so much on each lender's view of the country's prospects as it does on each lender's assessment of how other lenders may react to adverse developments elsewhere.

Banks have also tended to believe that they could limit their exposure to problem borrowers by withdrawing their maturing loans when difficulties arose. Thus banks have responded to uncertainty by shortening the maturity of their new commitments. For example, in the first half of 1982, when banks lent Mexico $7.3 billion, at least 60 percent of those loans had a maturity of under one year. Apparently the banks assumed that the funds could be withdrawn if economic conditions continued to deteriorate.[40] This way of operating does not, of course, lead to security, since the circumstances that induce one bank to retract its loans are likely to induce others to do the same. Such attempted withdrawals merely precipitate debt-servicing difficulties in the country concerned. Nevertheless, the presence of many—often several hundred—unrelated creditors gives each an incentive to withdraw if it can when serious problems arise.

The reliance of banks on such uncertain methods for reducing risk in international lending directly affects market stability. Unlike the situation in domestic markets, lenders have little or no control over the total indebtedness that countries may incur. Therefore, banks have no way to ensure that a borrowing country's financial condition will not deteriorate markedly during the term of a loan because of subsequent lending by more aggressive institutions. Lacking other sources of protection, bank creditors are tempted to withdraw their short-term and maturing

---

ble?" *Quarterly Review* (Federal Reserve Bank of New York, Summer 1981), pp. 10–20; Eaton and Gersovitz, "LDC Participation in International Financial Markets"; and Ingo Walter, "Country Risk, Portfolio Decisions and Regulation in International Bank Lending," *Journal of Banking and Finance*, vol. 5 (March 1981), pp. 77–92.

40. For an explanation of the buildup in short-term Mexican debt, see Pedro-Pablo Kuczynski, "Latin American Debt," *Foreign Affairs*, vol. 61 (Winter 1982–83), p. 348. It is also likely that borrowers preferred acquiring short-term debt to minimize borrowing costs.

loans when they anticipate an interruption in debt servicing. Under such circumstances the pricing mechanism also tends to break down: once credit rationing sets in, countries can no longer attract new funds by accepting higher spreads on their loans and are thus effectively shut out of the credit markets.[41] The lesson to be learned from recent events, therefore, is that the market cannot be expected to absorb severe shocks any more than it can be relied on in more normal times to impose a prudent ceiling on the indebtedness of individual countries.

The Role of Economic Recovery

The global recession of 1981–82 clearly contributed to the financial distress of borrowers in developing countries. To alleviate that stress, Western economic recovery is needed. Forecasts recently published by the Morgan Guaranty Trust Company are useful in evaluating how important recovery might be.[42] The base-case scenario in these forecasts (table 9) assumes that adjustment in developing countries takes place during a moderate recovery in OECD countries. The other scenarios examine the sensitivity of the base-case calculations in table 10 to assumptions about OECD recovery, terms of trade in developing countries, oil prices, and interest rates. These alternative scenarios have widely differing implications for the current account deficits and therefore for the funding needs of the major borrowers. These twenty-one countries had a total debt of about $514 billion outstanding at the end of 1982, equal to 178 percent of their exports. Their collective current account deficit was $61 billion in 1982, representing approximately 22 percent of exports. Furthermore, as of December 1982 their debt outstanding to Western banks was $303.3 billion, or 83.6 percent of all bank debt of developing countries.[43]

41. As recently as April 1982 a high-level task force on international bank lending, in a report to the IMF/World Bank Development Committee, suggested that "the pricing mechanism in international lending is functioning." The report concluded: "Developing-country borrowers with adequate policies and reasonable growth prospects are not likely to be denied continued market access solely because exogenous factors—such as a deterioration in their terms of trade or the adverse impact on debt service of high world interest rates—may have rendered their circumstances somewhat more problematic in the short run." See Task Force on Non-concessional Flows, "Final Report to the Development Committee" (IMF/World Bank, April 5, 1982), p. 19.

42. "Global Debt: Assessment and Long-Term Strategy," *World Financial Markets* (New York: Morgan Guaranty Trust, 1983), pp. 1–15.

43. Bank for International Settlements, *Maturity Distribution of International Bank Lending* (Basle, Switzerland: BIS, 1983).

Table 9. *Financing Scenarios for Major Developing-Country Borrowers*[a]
Percent per year unless otherwise specified

Item	1983	1984	1985	1986–90 (annual average)	1990
OECD real GNP growth	2.00	3.5	3.5	3.0	. . .
OECD inflation (dollar terms)	4.00	8.0	8.0	6.0	. . .
Bank cost of funds[b]	9.25	8.5	9.0	9.0	. . .
Oil prices (dollars a barrel, OPEC average)	28.00	29.0	32.0	0.0[c]	. . .
Change in non-oil commodity prices					
All non-oil commodities	2	12	10	1.4[c]	. . .
Foods	−2	11	8	2.0[c]	. . .
Industrial products	13	15	12	0.0[c]	. . .
Current account deficit					
Billions of dollars	41	27	28	. . .	34
Share of exports (percent)	15	9	8	. . .	5
Total debt					
Billions of dollars	557	582	619	. . .	822
Share of exports (percent)	196	182	166	. . .	123

Source: "Global Debt: Assessment and Long-Term Strategy," *World Financial Markets* (New York: Morgan Guaranty Trust, 1983), tables 5, 6, and 7.

a. Argentina, Brazil, Chile, Colombia, Ecuador, Mexico, Peru, Venezuela, Indonesia, Malaysia, the Philippines, South Korea, Taiwan, Thailand, Algeria, Egypt, Israel, Ivory Coast, Morocco, Nigeria, and Turkey.

b. London Interbank Offered Rate (six-month Eurodollar deposit rate).

c. Change in real (inflation-adjusted) prices, percent per year.

In the base-case scenario—adjustment in the developing countries and a moderate recovery in the OECD countries—over the next three years current account deficits would be halved to levels equivalent to only 8 percent of exports in 1985. This is a ratio typical of the period before the first oil shock. By the end of 1985 total debt would equal 166 percent of exports, a drop of over 15 percent from what the ratio is expected to be at the end of 1983. The ratio would continue falling gradually to 123 percent by 1990.

Table 10 details the implications of this scenario for the external debt and the debt-exports ratios of ten major borrowers. Although Brazil and Mexico remain the two largest borrowers in absolute magnitude, several noticeable shifts in the rankings are expected to occur during the 1980s. South Korea is expected to become the third largest developing-country borrower by 1985, surpassing Argentina. This will probably not cause problems for Korea, however, since its debt-exports ratio will most likely drop slightly during this time. In this scenario, Venezuela and Indonesia will hold third and fourth places by 1990, largely because of oil market conditions. Finally, Argentina and Chile are expected to show

Table 10. *Projections of External Debt of Major Developing-Country Borrowers*

Country or countries	Total (billions of dollars)[a]			Share of exports (percent)[b]		
	1982	1985	1990	1982	1985	1990
Twenty-one developing countries	514.0	619.0	822.0	178	166	123
Argentina	38.8	44.7	44.6	388	302	179
Brazil	86.3	104.7	121.9	345	333	219
Chile	17.2	17.8	17.7	285	187	116
Colombia	10.2	11.1	14.4	186	183	132
Mexico	84.6	95.5	116.7	253	199	124
Venezuela	33.2	37.5	69.6	155	190	213
Indonesia	21.9	33.4	52.9	98	135	133
Philippines	20.7	25.0	30.6	233	197	143
South Korea	37.2	47.0	50.5	121	111	64
Turkey	22.6	25.7	33.7	226	184	130

Source: "Global Debt: Assessment and Long-Term Strategy," *World Financial Markets*, table 6.
a. End of period.
b. Average debt for year as a share of exports of goods and services.

the most improvement among borrowers by 1990, while Venezuela will suffer the greatest deterioration.

The sensitivity of the above calculations to the base-case assumptions, particularly about OECD growth, are important (table 11). A decrease of 1 percent in the OECD real growth rate beginning in 1984 would increase the current account deficits and outstanding debt of the countries. External debt would increase to $632 billion by 1985 and $1,055 billion by 1990, and the debt-exports ratios would stay virtually constant. This outcome seems untenable because the required net new financing would be hard for borrowers to find in the face of such a bleak economic outlook. An increase of 1 percent in real growth, on the other hand, would vastly improve the developing countries' debt situations. Such an increase, however, would require an unusually strong and prolonged recovery in the industrial countries.

The sensitivity of these calculations to oil prices is also interesting. For the major borrowers the net effect of higher oil prices is favorable; that is, the gains for the oil exporters exceed the losses incurred by the oil importers. Finally, a rise in interest rates would hurt developing-country borrowers, while improved terms of trade would help them.

The base-case scenario requires $105 billion in new credits from all sources during 1983–85, a growth rate of about 6.4 percent a year. If

Table 11. *External Debt of Major Developing-Country Borrowers: Sensitivity to Base-Case Assumptions*[a]

Item	Total (billions of dollars)[b]			Share of exports (percent)[c]		
	1982	1985	1990	1982	1985	1990
Base case	514	619	882	178	166	123
Change in OECD real GNP growth rate						
+1 percent per year	...	605	568	...	158	80
−1 percent per year	...	632	1055	...	174	173
Change in terms of trade,						
+1 percent per year	...	608	660	...	164	102
Change in oil prices,						
+20 percent per year	...	600	687	...	154	99
Change in bank cost of funds,[d] +2 percent per year	...	640	930	...	170	137

Source: "Global Debt: Assessment and Long-Term Strategy," *World Financial Markets*, table 7.
a. Changes in assumptions apply from 1984.
b. End of period.
c. Average debt for year as a share of exports of goods and services.
d. London Interbank Offered Rate.

bank debt also grew at this rate, banks would have to extend about $62 billion in net new funds between December 1982 and December 1985. This would cover part, but not all, of the interest they were due. Furthermore, this base-case scenario assumes that debt will grow slightly more than 6 percent a year until 1990. Such a growth rate implies that banks would have to extend $180 billion in net new credits during the rest of this decade. The hope would be that banks would continue to reschedule debts now and that, once debt approached more normal levels, private capital markets would again consider developing countries creditworthy. The current extraordinary financing arrangements could then be phased out.

Given the problems that have already occurred in negotiations during the current reschedulings begun in 1982, however, it is clear that the need for new funds over the next three years (and for a long time thereafter) could make the rescheduling process difficult. In addition, the Morgan Guaranty calculations, by lumping the major Latin American borrowers together with other developing-country borrowers, mask the severe problems facing Latin America. For example, while the twenty-one major borrowers together had a debt-exports ratio of 178 percent in 1982, the eight Latin American borrowers had a ratio near 260 percent, the six Asian borrowers a ratio near 100 percent, and the other seven countries a ratio of about 170 percent.[44] Also, six of the eight Latin American debtors had ratios over 200 percent (Argentina's was 388 percent), while only one Asian borrower (the Philippines) had a ratio that high.[45] According to the calculations, Argentina and Brazil would still have ratios exceeding 300 percent in 1985. Finally, while the Morgan Guaranty forecasts are not explicit on this point, in the base-case scenario the 1985 and 1990 debt-exports ratios for the twenty-one major borrowers are the average of a high debt-exports ratio for Latin American borrowers balanced by a lower ratio for Asian borrowers.[46] It may therefore be hard to convince banks that three years of moderate economic recovery will make the Latin American borrowers attractive risks.

These calculations imply that a global recovery will ease the funding problems of developing countries. Even with a recovery, however, the next few years will still be difficult, because the need for substantial new inflows of funds for developing countries will still exist. Economic recovery is necessary, but it will not by itself resolve the current debt situation.

The Role of the International Monetary Fund

The IMF has supervised international financial arrangements and balance-of-payments adjustment since it was established at the end of World War II. It already has the authority to make loans to help member nations correct payments imbalances. Its procedures emphasize the temporary and conditional nature of these loans.[47] Thus many current proposals for handling the debt situation include a role for the IMF.

44. "Global Debt: Assessment and Long-Term Strategy," pp. 3–4 and chart 2.
45. Ibid., tables 5, 6.
46. According to forecasts, in 1985 at least six Latin American borrowers will exceed the average debt-exports ratio of the twenty-one major borrowers. Only two smaller borrowers, Peru and Ecuador, could have below-average ratios. In 1990 five of the Latin American borrowers are expected to exceed the overall average of 123 percent, Chile falling slightly below that. Ibid., table 6.
47. The conditionality of access to Fund resources has long been a topic of debate, but a standard practice has evolved over time. Limited borrowing remains possible with little or no conditionality, but countries wishing to borrow large sums (relative to their quotas) must submit to more conditionality. Low conditionality requires the existence of a balance-of-payments deficit and a declaration that measures are being taken to resolve the problem. High conditionality requires the country's design of a specific program to reduce the deficit, IMF agreement that the program is adequate, and a firm commitment to implement the program. For further discussion, see John Williamson, *The Lending Policies of the International Monetary Fund* (Washington, D.C.: Institute for International Economics, 1982), pp. 11–21.

IMF members contribute to its resources in proportion to their membership quotas, based roughly on the members' economic power. Quotas, which have been reviewed periodically since the founding of the Fund, currently account for SDR 61 billion (roughly $66 billion).[48] In February 1983 IMF members agreed to an increase in quotas of almost 50 percent (to SDR 90 billion, or $98 billion) subject to approval by the governments involved. The industrialized nations have also agreed to an enlargement and revision of the General Arrangements to Borrow (GAB).[49] The funds available would be expanded from the current SDR 6.4 billion (about $7 billion) to SDR 17 billion (about $19 billion). According to the agreement, Switzerland would join the GAB and the IMF would be able to draw on GAB resources to fund loans to any IMF member.

Because members will pay three-fourths of their quota increases in local currencies, the IMF will not be able to use a significant part of the new funds. However, the quota increase will provide about $15 billion in usable currencies. This is in addition to the $12 billion the expansion of the GAB will provide and the more than $4 billion available as a final installment of the 1981 credit line from Saudi Arabia to the Fund. Thus, the proposed changes would increase usable IMF resources by as much as $30 billion to $35 billion, of which the United States' contribution would be almost $8.5 billion.

Although it is difficult to judge the adequacy of the proposed quota increases, they—along with an increase in GAB resources—seem necessary for the next five years. (The IMF's rules provide for quota reviews at least every five years.) The Fund is likely to acquire large commitments over the next few years.[50] Furthermore, the full amount of the credit

48. The Special Drawing Right (SDR) is a composite currency used to denominate IMF transactions with its members; its components are the dollar, the deutsche mark, the yen, the British pound, and the French franc. The value of one SDR averaged $1.09 in the first three months of 1983.

49. For details on the quota increase, see "Executive Board Sends Report to Governors on Quota Increases Under Eighth Review," *IMF Survey* (March 7, 1983), p. 66. On the expanded GAB, see "Fund's Executive Board Approves the Revision, Enlargement of the GAB," *IMF Survey* (March 7, 1983), p. 68.

50. Brazil, for example, is counting on the IMF for SDR 4.96 billion ($5.4 billion) in addition to the net new money extended by the banks; Mexico is expecting SDR 3.41 billion ($3.9 billion); Argentina, SDR 1.5 billion ($1.64 billion); and Venezuela, $1.2 billion. See "Fund Approves Package of Assistance for Brazil Totaling SDR 5 Billion," *IMF Survey* (March 7, 1983), p. 65; and "Commitments to Members Show a Sharp Rise: Total

lines promised to the IMF under the GAB facility and the 1981 Saudi credit line may not be available if some of the countries involved are experiencing balance-of-payments difficulties themselves. Indeed, the IMF may have to find more resources soon, in which case it may turn to private markets. A recent study has suggested that the Fund approach these markets now for relatively small sums to facilitate rapid mobilization of market finance in case of later need.[51] Regular borrowing from private markets would represent a change in philosophy for the IMF, however, since such borrowing would conflict with the IMF's traditional emphasis on quotas as its primary funding source.

The IMF as Manager of New Credits

The IMF is also now engaged in a new type of international credit management, evident in both the Mexican and Brazilian reschedulings. For the first time the IMF has insisted that the banks increase their loans outstanding as part of a package including IMF loans and IMF-approved stabilization plans in the borrowing countries. One important aspect of these rescheduling packages has been the Fund's efforts to persuade banks not to cut their interbank credit lines to commercial and central banks from developing countries.[52] By requiring the banks to extend net new funds, these coordinated negotiations have removed the fear that developing countries would use IMF funds to pay back the banks without helping developing countries out of their funding problems.

The major change in the Fund's role in the recent reschedulings, compared with commercial reschedulings of the 1970s, has been its willingness to provide banks with more detailed guidelines on their part of the financing package. Previously the banks and the IMF had negotiated separately with the debtor, the banks making their rescheduling conditional on an IMF-approved adjustment plan. Banks have wanted

SDR 6.9 Billion in Two-Month Period," *IMF Survey* (March 21, 1983), p. 89. See also Alan Friedman, "Venezuela Seeking 3-Month Delay on Debt," *Financial Times*, March 23, 1983.

51. Group of Thirty, *The International Monetary Fund and the Private Markets* (New York: Group of Thirty, 1983).

52. In the Brazilian package, for example, the IMF demanded four things from the banks: new funds of $4.4 billion, rollover for eight years of $4 billion in principal falling due in 1983, maintenance of short-term trade credits at $8.8 billion, and restoration of interbank lines to the $7.5 billion level. See Peter Montagnon and Andrew Whitley, "IMF Brazil Loan to Proceed despite Credit Lines Delay," *Financial Times*, February 21, 1983; and Whitley and Montagnon, "Brazil's Jumbo Loan Agreement Due for Signing Today," *Financial Times*, February 25, 1983.

an IMF "seal of approval," at least since the Peruvian reschedulings of 1976–78, when an attempt to negotiate an adjustment program without the IMF's involvement ended in failure.[53] The Western nations that provide funds also find it useful to have the IMF coordinate temporary support operations.

The next few years may provide a severe test of the IMF seal of approval. Brazil and Chile have already been in at least temporary violation of the guidelines in their stabilization program. The Fund must somehow enforce its guidelines when necessary, yet still be able to adjust its programs to changing conditions in the borrower's country without undermining IMF credibility with banks and creditor nations.

Information Sharing

Bankers have argued that the debt problem has been caused largely by the lack of adequate information on debtors. The IMF, on the other hand, is often assumed to have more extensive information on countries, especially on total outstanding debt and debt service, because it constantly monitors the economies of its member countries. A variety of proposals suggest that the IMF make its data and internal economic projections available to banks or that IMF officials meet regularly with bankers to share information.[54]

The effects of such information sharing on the relationship between the IMF and its member countries will have to be evaluated carefully. Temporarily, of course, some sharing can probably be justified by the current methods for arranging new credits during reschedulings, but in the longer run there are several obstacles that must be overcome. For example, if a country does not want certain information made public, it might make even less information available to the IMF than it normally would. There is also the question of what information should be exchanged. It might be limited to raw numbers on a few parameters, such

53. Irving S. Friedman, "The Role of Private Banks in Stabilization Programs," in William R. Cline and Sidney Weintraub, eds., *Economic Stabilization in Developing Countries* (Brookings Institution, 1981), pp. 235–65.

54. For a sampling of comments, see Lawrence Rout, "Some Commercial Banks Press the IMF to Provide Data on Borrowing Nations," *Wall Street Journal*, April 1, 1983; "Program for Improved Supervision and Regulation of International Lending," Joint Memorandum presented by the Comptroller of the Currency, Federal Deposit Insurance Corporation and the Federal Reserve Board to the House Committee on Banking, Finance and Urban Affairs, April 7, 1983, pp. 8–9 (hereafter "Joint Memorandum on International Lending").

as total debt or the ratio of debt to exports in a country, or it might go so far as to include assessments of debt capacity. Finally, problems would result if the IMF had to deal with each bank individually. To the extent that information sharing is hampered by coordination problems, the recently formed Institute of International Finance (which grew out of the meetings of bankers known as the Ditchley group) may be able to serve as a liaison. An alternative would be for the Institute itself to collect the information that private banks need on debtors, so that IMF data could remain confidential.

The IMF as Assessor of Debt Capacity

Analysts have also suggested that the IMF be more active in monitoring balance-of-payments financing by developing guidelines on the appropriate size and composition of member countries' external debt.[55] Currently the Fund constrains a member country's borrowing practices only when funding problems have forced the borrower to apply for IMF assistance.

A more active role in debt surveillance would be an important policy departure for the IMF. Even if the Fund did not require new legal authority, such a change could not be implemented without the support of debtors, creditor countries, and the banks.[56] Even more of a problem would be the political question of fair play: for developing countries to accept willingly IMF guidance on external loans, government deficits, and exchange-rate policy, it might be necessary for industrial nations, including the United States, to be subject to such review. Other difficulties might include guidelines not always being followed or, if they were followed, the expectation that the IMF would extricate banks if debtor countries could not meet their obligations. Finally, a better understanding of what constitutes sustainable debt capacity would have to be developed before the IMF could assume such a surveillance role.[57] If

55. See Anthony M. Solomon, president of the Federal Reserve Bank of New York, "Restoring Balance in an Interdependent World," remarks before the Bicentennial Financial Symposium, October 7, 1982, pp. 10–14; and "Joint Memorandum on International Lending," pp. 8–9.

56. The IMF is presently required by article 4 of its Articles of Agreement to exercise firm surveillance on members' exchange-rate policies, a surveillance authority that presumably could be extended without formal amendment to embrace external debt management, on the grounds that external debt has important exchange-rate implications.

57. For an analysis of the question of debt capacity, see Donogh C. McDonald, "Debt Capacity and Developing Country Borrowing: A Survey of the Literature," *IMF Staff Papers*, vol. 29 (December 1982), pp. 603–46.

these problems could be resolved, such a role could compensate for the lack of enforceable conditionality in international lending.

Regulatory Constraints on Banks

The perception that banks have been too expansionary in their international lending has led to several regulatory proposals designed to slow it down. Such restrictions can be justified on three grounds. First, until now financial markets and particularly equity investors have lacked the information to determine whether banks are taking excessive risks. Second, existing protective regulation in the form of deposit insurance and lender-of-last-resort arrangements may have further undermined market discipline in international lending. Finally, the heavy social costs of bank failure could justify official curbs that go beyond the market's restraints on risk taking.

Since the immediate crisis calls for more international lending than the market seems willing to provide, new regulatory constraints on banks might complicate stabilization unless the constraints are well formulated and carefully implemented. It is also important that regulations be coordinated internationally.

The first five options outlined below should probably be regarded as complementary, although in most discussions two of them—reserves provisions and capital-adequacy requirements—are treated as alternatives. Among current legislative proposals, one Senate bill combines new capital-adequacy standards with mandatory reserves provisions but leaves the manner in which these are to be applied to the discretion of the Federal Reserve System.[58] This is in line with the program federal regulatory agencies have jointly proposed, which imposes mandatory reserves provisions, increases disclosure requirements, and includes foreign exposures in capital-adequacy standards, but avoids country-lending limits.[59]

Limits on Country Lending

Country-lending limits are usually proposed in the form of a specified maximum exposure to any one country measured as a percentage of the

58. The Senate bill (S.695, 98 Cong. 1 sess.) was approved on June 8, 1983, by a 55–34 vote. *Congressional Record*, daily edition (June 8, 1983), pp. S7916–20.
59. "Joint Memorandum on International Lending."

lending bank's capital. Besides providing a crude but effective way to force banks to diversify, country-lending limits would restrict the leverage that countries with large loans might gain over the lending bank. Also, once a bank lends so much to a country that the country's default would threaten the lender's solvency, the bank has less incentive to refrain from further lending, since the incremental risk incurred is minimal.[60] Finally, as a general principle, it seems undesirable that one country's default should be able to threaten the stability of another country's domestic banking system.

Objections to a uniform lending limit applied to all countries include the fact that such a limit would ignore the varying credit needs of large and small countries as well as the widely differing credit standing of sovereign borrowers. A uniform limit could also prove disruptive to several countries, such as Canada, Japan, and the United Kingdom, where U.S. banks have substantial claims, often over 100 percent of the banks' capital. Finally, regulators have argued that the transitional arrangements that would be needed to implement a uniform country-lending limit would take so long that they would undermine the scheme's credibility.[61] A differentiated limit based on the perceived weakness of individual countries would probably be impractical, given the short time in which a country's financial status can change and the inability of banks, collectively, to adjust their lending policies to changing conditions. Differentiated limits could also be destabilizing if publicized changes in limits provoked strong market reactions to the country concerned.

Although uniform country-lending limits would force banks to diversify their international lending most effectively, many banks would already have loans well over any reasonable limit if such a scheme were introduced now. That situation would require either a sudden and undesirable contraction of international lending or a lengthy transitional period. Nevertheless, related problems could be partly resolved if country-lending limits were combined with increased capital-adequacy requirements.

---

60. This is explored further in Jack M. Guttentag and Richard J. Herring, "Uncertainty and Insolvency Exposure by International Banks" (University of Pennsylvania, Wharton School, June 1983), pp. 6–16.

61. See "Joint Memorandum on International Lending," p. 9; and "Statement of C. T. Conover, Comptroller of the Currency, to the Subcommittee on International Finance of the Senate Committee on Banking, Housing and Urban Affairs," February 17, 1983, pp. 27–29.

Capital-Adequacy Requirements

Some countries, particularly in Europe, impose formal capital-adequacy requirements incorporating specific weights for certain types of risk exposure. This regulatory approach could be adapted to take into account country risk, although it would be difficult to determine what weights should be applied. In the United States, capital-adequacy assessments are more informal than in Europe. However, it seems desirable at least to reverse the anomalous situation in which those banks (the multinationals) with the largest exposures also tend to have the lowest capital ratios.[62] Requiring banks to increase their capital against prospective losses is one of the few regulatory initiatives that strengthens the banking system in both the short and the long run.

The U.S. regulatory authorities have proposed including country-exposure concentrations in their assessment of capital adequacy.[63] If the marginal cost of the capital required to cover high levels of exposure proves prohibitive, banks would cut back on such lending. In those circumstances, the effects of capital-adequacy requirements would be similar to those of country-lending limits. Guidelines that explicitly account for country-exposure concentrations have not yet been developed. The Federal Reserve Board has, however, recently issued new capital standards for the seventeen multinational banks. These guidelines, which require the multinational banks to maintain primary capital equal to 5 percent or more of total assets, have been described as part of the regulators' response to the foreign activities of American banks.[64]

Reserves Provisions

In the United States, banks hold reserves called the "allowance for possible loan losses" as a buffer—in addition to equity, retained earnings, and other capital—against potential loan losses. These reserves include funds set aside to cover possible losses on doubtful loans as well as to cover unexpected losses. Currently, banks and their auditors determine what, if any, provisions should be made against prospective losses

62. It may be argued that larger banks have greater opportunities for risk diversification than smaller banks and should, therefore, be expected to have lower capital ratios. But there is no domestic counterpart to the risk concentrations in international lending. For example, domestic agricultural and energy-related lending usually requires collateral.

63. See "Joint Memorandum on International Lending," especially p. 4 and app. A.

64. Kenneth B. Noble, "Fed Sets Capital Rules Affecting 5 Large Banks," *New York Times*, June 14, 1983.

on international loans. However, the lack of standardized accounting procedures in this area raises some problems. First, widely differing accounting practices among banks and national banking systems may distort competition in international lending. Second, to maintain public confidence, it is necessary to safeguard the integrity of bank accounting systems by ensuring that published accounts reflect, so far as possible, market realities. And, most important, banks may incur excessive risks if reported profits and balance sheet totals are not adjusted for probable losses. International lending poses particular problems because risks are seldom realized but instead are cumulated and deferred through the rescheduling process. Therefore, loan quality can deteriorate without this being reflected in banks' published accounts.

Various proposals would require banks to make either general or specific provisions against their international loan portfolios. One approach is to penalize rescheduled or nonperforming loans; another is to impose graduated requirements calculated on the basis of a bank's loan concentrations in individual countries; and a third approach is to vary the requirements according to each country's assessed credit standing.[65] An alternative to the last approach would be to require banks to provision some part of the spread charged on loans to foreign borrowers, on the principle that the spread incorporates a risk premium that should not be reported as profit.

U.S. regulatory authorities have proposed that countries with protracted debt-servicing problems should be classified as reservable.[66] Bank loans to such countries would then be subject to an initial provision of 10 percent, with additional annual provisions of 15 percent if warranted. As presently formulated, this scheme would require the authorities to exercise some discretion in determining whether a country should be classified as reservable.

Both mandatory provisions and more stringent capital requirements seek to recognize country risk. Provisioning attempts to quantify prospective losses. But such quantification is particularly hazardous in relation to country exposure, for the risk on these loans is essentially one of repudiation, and therefore "all or nothing." Furthermore, mandatory provisioning, in today's uncertain banking climate, could encourage banks to withdraw altogether from international lending. Reg-

65. Proposals contained in Henry C. Wallich, "International Lending and the Role of Bank Supervisory Cooperation," remarks at the International Conference of Banking Supervisors, Washington, D.C., September 24, 1981; "Statement of C. T. Conover," p. 29; and S. Res. 502, 98 Cong. 1 sess., February 16, 1983.
66. See "Joint Memorandum on International Lending," pp. 6–7 and app. C.

ulatory agencies, therefore, should be given the authority to implement reserves provisions using their own discretion. Otherwise these provisions might interfere with the attempt to maintain an orderly flow of credit to the major developing-country borrowers, and thereby add to the difficulties already facing the regulatory authorities in their search for a resolution of both short- and long-term aspects of the crisis.

Disclosure

A strong case can be made for disclosure by banks of their country-risk exposures on two separate grounds: bank shareholders and creditors have a right to know how their funds are being used; and such disclosure would enable financial markets to discipline banks incurring excessive risks. Disclosure would also ease the responsibilities of regulatory authorities who now supervise international lending without requiring banks to divulge their practices to the marketplace. However, compelling banks to reveal their country-risk exposure in a crisis atmosphere could complicate the immediate task of ensuring adequate credit flows to country borrowers. And disclosure requirements would need to be coordinated internationally so that U.S. banks would not be placed at a competitive disadvantage.

U.S. regulators have proposed that banks disclose loans to individual countries exceeding 1 percent of total assets, along with information on the type of borrower (banks, public-sector entities, and others) and the maturity distribution of loans. For those countries where exposure is between 0.75 percent and 1 percent of total assets, only the total loans outstanding would be listed.[67] Such a disclosure requirement would enable financial markets to appraise the riskiness of banks' international loan portfolios more realistically than has been possible so far.

Accounting for Fees

U.S. regulatory authorities have also recently prepared a set of procedures that would standardize the accounting for fees. In addition to the stated interest payments on syndicated international loans, banks generally charge certain fees for the credit. Some of these fees cover the costs of arranging or administering a credit, others cover the costs of providing a credit line for a prescribed time, and others are front-end fees designed solely to increase the effective yield of the loan. Banks

67. Ibid., pp. 5–6 and app. B.

now account for such fees in a variety of ways. Standardization proposals would divide fees—except those that reimburse costs—over the life of the loan when calculating earnings.[68]

In the past, banks treated front-end fees as income as soon as the loan was closed, which may have led banks to promote international loans to boost reported earnings. The new rules would encourage more prudent practices. The change, however, would have only a temporary effect on bank earnings.[69] Therefore, it would probably not have any significant long-term effect on borrowers or lenders, although it could accentuate the problem of keeping banks lending over the short term.

Regulation of the Euromarkets

Other proposals to regulate the Eurocurrency markets on prudential grounds are not directly relevant to international lending by U.S. banks, since this lending is already monitored by U.S. supervisory authorities on a worldwide consolidated basis. Concerns remain, however, about the banks with headquarters in other countries that in some cases have been able to escape domestic surveillance of their international operations by routing such business through offshore markets. These competing offshore financial centers that solicit business from the international banking community raise serious issues that need to be addressed.[70] On the other hand, proposals for broad reform of the offshore banking markets are best considered separately from those relating to the present international debt problem.

Changes in the Terms and Sources of Commercial Lending

Various changes in the sources and terms of commercial financing available to developing countries have been suggested in recent years. These suggestions are usually based on a belief that the standard contract

68. Ibid., p. 7 and app. D.

69. For example, suppose a bank extended $1 billion in four-year loans every year, charging 1 percent in fees. The traditional method of including all fees as current income would allow the bank to declare $10 million in underwriting earnings every year, beginning in the first year. Averaging would require the bank to report $2.5 million, $5 million, and $7.5 million in underwriting earnings in years one, two, and three, and $10 million in every succeeding year. Thus the choice of method has a short-term effect on reported earnings but no long-term effect.

70. See, for example, Richard S. Dale, "International Banking Is Out of Control," *Challenge* (January–February 1983), pp. 14–19.

between banks and borrowers allows too much variability in payments or too short a maturity for borrowers' needs. This section examines a few of the commercial alternatives to the floating-rate, fixed-maturity bank loans now prevalent in international lending.

When nominal interest rates rise unexpectedly, borrowers have to make greater-than-anticipated payments on their loans. If the increase in interest rates were matched exactly by an increase in inflation, then (other things being equal) the real value of the payments over the life of the loan would remain the same. However, the increase in nominal payments effectively shortens the average maturity of the loan, forces the country to enter the market more often to fund the same amount of real debt, and may thereby increase the likelihood of reschedulings.

One proposed solution to this problem is the flexible-maturity loan.[71] Interest rates would still be set at a margin over LIBOR, but the annual debt-service payments would be predetermined. The difference between the annual payment and the interest charges would contribute to repayment of the loan's principal, and payments at the contracted annual level would continue until all the principal was repaid. An escape clause in the loan agreement would have to state that payments must cover the interest due.

A flexible-maturity loan is similar to several types of home mortgage agreements already used to a limited extent in the U.S. market.[72] Such a loan protects borrowers from unexpected increases in nominal interest rates that temporarily raise the share of income devoted to interest payments.[73] It also allows borrowers to smooth the adjustment to real interest-rate shocks that increase interest payments but do not affect income or exports directly.

Although the flexible-maturity loan would probably be attractive to borrowers, lenders might find it unacceptable. Like the traditional floating-rate loan in international lending, it does limit the banks' risk caused by rising interest rates. On the other hand, banks may be less satisfied with an implied reduction in their liquidity. The automatic extension of maturity may also lessen the ability of banks or international

71. Laurie S. Goodman, "An Alternative to Rescheduling LDC Debt in an Inflationary Environment," *Columbia Journal of World Business*, vol. 17 (Spring 1982), pp. 20–27.
72. Ibid.
73. For example, in the traditional loan, if the expected interest rate had been 10 percent but inflation jumped 5 percent, interest payments would increase 50 percent immediately. Under the same conditions, the value of exports would increase only 5 percent.

organizations to control borrowers when adjustment measures are called for.

Another way to avoid unexpected changes in the face value of loan repayments due to unexpected changes in interest rates is to use fixed-rate rather than floating-rate loans. Fixed-rate loans, however, make the real value of interest payments uncertain, so they are not necessarily better for borrowers or lenders. Because an unexpected rise in nominal interest rates (perhaps because of inflation) would decrease the real value of the payments, countries sometimes might benefit from fixed-rate loans, in this case at the expense of banks. But though unexpected increases in interest rates would reduce the real debt burden on fixed-rate loans far more than on floating-rate loans,[74] a decline in rates would make already contracted fixed-rate loans more expensive than floating-rate funds. Fixed-rate loans also expose the banks to considerable funding risk, which they do not bear with floating-rate loans. Therefore, a switch to fixed-rate loans would probably be a move in the wrong direction.

The international lending system does require alternative sources of long-term financing, since the term of a bank loan rarely exceeds eight years because of the bank's need for liquidity. The suitability of long-term finance to the borrower's needs is a key factor when considering potential financing sources. While the long lead times on development projects make long-term financing desirable, trade financing, for example, should be covered by short-term loans that match the maturity of the underlying transaction. Finally, balance-of-payments loans designed to help a country adjust to unfavorable shocks, temporary or permanent, should also be short term, since temporary shocks require only temporary financing, and the real adjustment to permanent shocks should not be unduly delayed. In light of these considerations the authorities should not encourage a complete reliance on long-term financing, although it is necessary to lengthen the average maturity of financing for developing countries.

The two main sources of long-term funds potentially available for developing countries are direct investments and bonds. Country borrowers have tended to avoid both of these because the interest costs have seemed too high compared with those of bank loans. Countries have also feared that direct investments might offer foreigners control over a country's actions. If, because of current problems, debtors reconsider

74. Floating-rate loans, because they are adjusted quarterly or semi-annually, are more responsive to unexpected changes in interest rates.

these other commercial sources of long-term financing, direct investment would probably be preferable to bonds for several reasons. First, a large number of bondholders could complicate future reschedulings if they should occur. Second, direct investment offers greater opportunities for creditors and debtors to share risks and rewards as economic conditions change. It is also possible for foreign equity investors to suffer losses on a project without prompting other creditors to withdraw their funds from the country.[75] There is still a link between bonds or direct investments and a country's general capacity to pay, since the repatriation of profits or interest payments to foreign investors depends on the availability of foreign exchange. In any case, if countries find it either desirable or necessary to use longer-term sources of funding in the future, they will first have to reexamine the policies that discouraged use of these financing sources in the first place.

Debt Restructuring

If an unmanageable debt situation were to be resolved through unilateral defaults or repudiation rather than through debt relief, rescheduling, or the provision of new funds, then attention would immediately shift from protecting borrowers to protecting the banking system. As matters now stand, regulatory authorities cannot recapitalize U.S. banks on the scale that would be required if they were to incur large losses on foreign loans. The most probable outcome of such losses would be a decision by federal regulators to permit banks to write off delinquent foreign claims over an extended period, thereby preserving bank solvency for legal and supervisory purposes. It is not clear, however, that financial markets would readily accept this concept of solvency. In the meantime, banks would face a severe disruption of their cash flow and earnings. For this reason maintaining the creditworthiness of borrowers should be the main concern of policymakers.

The present emergency-lending practices are stopgap measures designed to sustain credit flows to developing nations and the solvency of the international banking system, pending a sustained global economic recovery. However, because the timing, pace, and duration of any recovery are uncertain, the need for more radical measures cannot be ruled out. Five contingency plans are considered here. They range from

75. This would also be true for bonds if cross-default clauses were not included in bond agreements.

outright debt relief to flexible rescheduling arrangements, risk transfers between banks and official institutions, and alternative ways to provide new funds to country borrowers.

Exchange Participation Notes

Under this scheme the central banks of debtor countries would issue exchange participation notes (EPNs) giving lenders proportional rights to some agreed-upon percentage of each country's total annual foreign-exchange receipts.[76] These rights, in the form of negotiable debt instruments, would replace repayments of principal to creditor banks, but interest payments would be made according to the original loan agreements. The scheme, which is similar to proposals suggested in the 1940s, is designed to tie a country's debt-service payments to its capacity to pay without providing any debt relief or transferring risks currently borne by banks.[77] In this case, capacity to pay is assessed in terms of a country's ability to repay a loan's principal in any one year rather than in terms of its ability to carry the debt over a longer period.

The scheme's main virtue is simplicity, but it may not offer significant advantages over present rescheduling arrangements or be acceptable either to banks or borrowers. Under the scheme, the maturity of banks' international loans would become indeterminate. This might not matter if an active secondary market in EPNs emerged but, because any resulting market price would be significantly below book value, banks would be reluctant to commit new funds after incurring losses on their existing international loan portfolios.

The EPN scheme, therefore, might cause banks to withdraw from international lending but does not provide debt relief or alternative sources of funding. This seems to contradict the scheme's basic assumptions that borrowers would still have "continued access to a reasonable volume of trade credits" and that the maintenance of interest payments would require substantial amounts of money "through the efforts of international institutions."[78] Finally, this scheme would require the

76. Norman A. Bailey, R. David Luft, and Roger W. Robinson, Jr., "Exchange Participation Notes: An Approach to the International Financial Crisis," in Thibaut de Saint Phalle, ed., *The International Financial Crisis: An Opportunity for Constructive Action* (Georgetown University, Center for Strategic and International Studies, 1983), pp. 27–36.
77. For a reference to the earlier proposals linking Latin American debt repayments to export proceeds, see H. C. Wallich, "The Future of Latin American Dollar Bonds," *American Economic Review*, vol. 33 (June 1943), p. 331.
78. Bailey and others, "Exchange Participation Notes," pp. 31–32.

monitoring of a country's foreign-exchange receipts and a level of involvement in the affairs of developing countries that would probably be resisted.

International Debt Discount Corporation

Under this scheme creditor governments would establish an International Debt Discount Corporation (IDDC) that would issue long-term bonds to banks in exchange for the banks' loans to developing countries.[79] The banks would be given a brief period to sell to the IDDC some specified percentage of all (not a selection of) their sovereign loans at a uniform discount of 10 percent of face value.[80] The IDDC would then be the holder of the discounted loans to developing countries. Loans acquired by the IDDC would be rescheduled on a long-term basis to conform to the maturity of its own liabilities. During rescheduling the IDDC could then pass on part of the discount directly to debtor countries as debt relief, although it could also provide relief by charging lower interest rates or granting grace periods before repayments of principal begin. The key elements in the proposal, therefore, are an optional transfer of risk at significant cost to the banks, modest debt relief for borrowers, and a stretching out of payments.

Two underlying premises of this asset-exchange proposal are that the debt burdens of developing countries must be reduced "so that they do not have to pursue domestic policies that jeopardize internal stability and interfere with worldwide recovery" and that banks should be able "to go on lending because developing countries must go on borrowing."[81] But new loans made by the banks after the initial period for discounting old loans would not be allowed into the IDDC if problems should arise again. Those banks that decided to take advantage of the IDDC option, however, would by implication be valuing their outstanding loans at more than 10 percent below book value. Not only would such banks presumably be unwilling to extend net new funds in the future, but they might also wish to withdraw old loans not transferred to the IDDC as those loans matured. On the other hand, nonparticipating banks would be given no incentive to engage in additional lending.

79. Peter B. Kenen, "A Bailout Plan for the Banks," *New York Times*, March 6, 1983; and Kenen, "Outline of a Proposal for an International Debt Discount Corporation" (Princeton University, May 3, 1983).

80. The Kenen proposal uses the figure 10 percent, although other discounts could be substituted without changing the scheme's principal elements.

81. Kenen, "A Bailout Plan for the Banks."

The fundamental objection to the IDDC proposal is that it not only offers little debt relief but also does nothing to encourage new bank lending to country borrowers and might even aggravate the tendency of banks to unwind previous loan commitments. Thus developing countries might continue to face severe funding difficulties. The scheme also involves the practical problems associated with creating a new institution, lacks the flexibility needed to cope with rapidly changing economic circumstances, and would involve governments in large commitments (though not cash outlays) they might be reluctant to assume.

A Worldwide MAC

Another possibility is a debt-restructuring scheme based on principles the Municipal Assistance Corporation (MAC) used to convert New York City's short-term debt into long-term debt.[82] Essentially, the scheme would involve creating an institution—a subsidiary of the World Bank or the IMF or a new institution guaranteed by Western governments— that could acquire banks' international loans in exchange for long-term (twenty-five- to thirty-year maturity) low-interest bonds. The new entity would become the substitute creditor to present country borrowers on this same long-term basis. The scheme differs from the IDDC proposal mainly in the degree of debt relief offered to borrowers: loans rescheduled through the worldwide MAC would carry a concessional interest rate of perhaps 6 percent, which might represent annual interest savings of between $15 billion and $20 billion. The substantial costs associated with this relief would be allocated—through negotiation—among taxpayers, countries, and bank stockholders.

The main features of this proposal, then, are long-term rescheduling combined with large-scale debt relief under a mandatory buy-out and risk-transfer arrangement that would impose considerable, though unspecified, losses on banks. The main benefit would be an immediate reduction in developing countries' external financing requirements. But, given the scale of losses implied, banks would almost certainly want to withdraw indefinitely from international lending. Furthermore, it would seem difficult to justify across-the-board debt relief irrespective of the particular circumstances of individual country debtors. Above all, the

82. Felix G. Rohatyn, "A Plan for Stretching Out Global Debt," *Business Week*, February 28, 1983, pp. 15–18. The restructuring of New York City's debt under the original MAC scheme was possible because the state allocated a tax-revenue stream to debt servicing that the city could not touch.

scheme would necessarily involve complex negotiations about the allocation of costs among the various parties involved as well as unprecedented government involvement in international financial markets.

Reduced Spreads

At the opposite end of the debt-relief spectrum, at least in terms of scale, is the proposal that banks should, under present circumstances, forgo the penalty lending margins or spreads that are applied to rescheduled debts.[83] Although the maturing debt of most sovereign borrowers usually carries an original spread of less than 1 percent, banks are requiring an additional premium of up to 2 percent as their price for agreeing to deferred repayment of principal. This additional risk premium could be dropped as a concession to hard-pressed borrowers, since by adding to the debt burden it may actually increase the risk of default. On the other hand, rescheduling terms are closely tied to the provision of new loans, and there is a danger that if rescheduling spreads were reduced, some banks—particularly smaller ones—might be less inclined to participate in new credit programs. Nevertheless, when relations between bank creditors and country debtors are becoming increasingly strained, a concession of this kind might yield benefits beyond the modest relief it offers borrowers.

Marginal Loan Guarantees

Most of the proposed debt-restructuring schemes focus on banks' old loans rather than on the need for new loans. Even during a moderate economic recovery, however, net new credits will have to be extended. Therefore, a case can be made for finding ways to sustain international credit flows while trying to lock in old loans. One approach would be for the IMF, or some other government-backed body, to formally guarantee new bank loans insofar as such loans are mandated under the IMF's own lending programs, on the condition that old loans be rescheduled.[84] The guarantees, which would apply only to net new credits, would be sold

83. See comments by Martin Feldstein, chairman of the Council of Economic Advisers, in Hobart Rowen, ''Banks Charging $800 Million for Help to Mexico,'' *Washington Post*, March 20, 1983.

84. The IMF now does not have explicit powers to guarantee loans. For this reason a new institution or some mechanism for cooperation among creditor nations might be needed.

to banks either at a uniform rate of 2 percent a year, for example, or at a variable rate linked to the borrower's credit standing. To show that banks were not being bailed out, old debt could be subordinated to the new; this already occurs under domestic corporate debt restructuring. This scheme's basic assumption is that the assurance of renewed credit flows would sustain the international financial system, pending an upturn in global economic activity. Initially there would be no debt relief and no losses imposed on banks, so they could continue to engage in international lending. If, however, the debt burden of developing countries were to become unmanageable because of unfavorable economic developments, the scheme could be adapted to provide debt relief—for instance, by having the banks write off some portion of their old loans over a period of time.

Marginal loan guarantees would inevitably involve some of the same organizational problems that establishing a discounting mechanism for international loans would create. On the other hand, the marginal-loan-guarantee scheme is more flexible and does not require Western governments to underwrite old loans. Marginal loan guarantees could be used to control the flow of new credits as rapidly changing economic conditions dictate. The objective, however, would be to allow market forces to take over again as soon as circumstances permitted.

A Comparison of Debt-Restructuring Schemes

Essentially there are two situations in which the present emergency-lending regime might become unmanageable. First, the minimum financial requirements (however judged) of debtor countries might begin to exceed the maximum amount that banks could reasonably lend. Some bankers have defined that limit as the point at which a bank's loans to developing countries, measured as a percentage of bank capital, would be increased.[85] A renewed funding shortfall could then precipitate widespread country defaults. Few debt-restructuring schemes specifically address the need for new money, and some might even reduce the amount of international credit available because of the losses these schemes impose on banks. Unlike the other proposals, however, mar-

85. In recent years the capital resources of U.S. banks have been increasing at an annual rate of about 10 percent, while current IMF credit programs usually call for an increase of 7 percent in bank lending to major country borrowers. Some bankers have indicated that they would not be willing to increase their capital exposure to individual countries. See, for instance, the statement by Barry Sullivan, chairman of the First National Bank of Chicago, cited in *Financial Times*, March 3, 1983.

ginal loan guarantees could be used to sustain the required level of international lending; presumably, funding shortfalls would disappear as economic conditions improved.

Present emergency arrangements would also be inadequate if debt burdens were too large for certain developing nations to carry. But because there is no widely accepted way to measure a country's debt capacity, and because that capacity, however measured, depends largely on global economic conditions, it would be wise to defer for as long as possible any initiatives to write off debts or implement concessional interest rates (other than reduced spreads). Such debt-relief measures would alter banks' perceptions of risk, possibly causing banks to withdraw from international lending for an extended period. In the long run this would perpetuate the present debt crisis and damage developing countries' access to credit markets. If debt relief eventually becomes unavoidable, it should allow for changing economic conditions and not be introduced as a one-time concession. In particular, the virtual halving of the developing countries' debt burdens called for by the worldwide MAC proposal could present severe transitional difficulties for the banking system, as well as formidable problems in allocating the costs of relief between banks and governments. The flexibility and gradualism that marginal loan guarantees offer are preferable to more dramatic proposals aimed at resolving the world debt problem in one fell swoop.

Summary and Conclusions

The scope and timing of the present debt crisis result largely from the protracted recession and accompanying high interest rates that have afflicted the world economy since 1979. Weaknesses in the international lending system, however, help explain both the market's failure to adapt to deteriorating economic conditions and the sudden breakdown of the market recycling mechanism in the summer of 1982.

One lesson to be learned from all this is that careful appraisal of individual country risks, coupled with geographic diversification of lending, gives banks little protection when contagious credit withdrawals hit borrowers in a particular region. The credit standing of countries depends as much on confidence as on objective criteria of debt capacity; in a free market the collective behavior of banks can cause considerable instability.

It is too early to say whether, after the traumas of 1982–83, most banks will want to stay in international lending. Even if the drop in oil prices and the beginnings of economic recovery moderate the demand for new credits, banks may want to play a much smaller role in financing developing countries than they have in the recent past. If so, the present emergency-lending regime may have to continue for several more years. Nevertheless, it is necessary to consider what might stabilize international credit markets in the future. Hastily conceived measures to prevent recent events from recurring could complicate the immediate task of sustaining the flow of international credit. There is also a danger that radical initiatives could irreparably damage international credit markets over the longer term.

Under the present emergency-lending regime, the IMF's role in coordinating international credit programs is central. To maintain that role IMF resources—quotas and the GAB facility—should be increased as proposed by the IMF's Interim Committee. If a prompt and sustained global economic recovery does not occur, however, major new initiatives may be needed. Various debt-relief and official buy-out schemes have been proposed to deal with such an eventuality, but any moves in this direction could cut off new bank credit indefinitely and thus harm third world borrowers. For this reason policymakers should consider guarantees for new bank lending. This scheme is not a bailout, since the guarantees would be sold to banks at a premium and the old debt would be subordinated to the new. Such a scheme could be applied flexibly in a rapidly changing economic climate and later adapted to some form of debt relief should this become unavoidable. In the meantime, by reducing spreads on rescheduled debts, banks themselves could help ease the pressures on developing-country borrowers, while still upholding the sanctity of contractual obligations.

Longer-term structural reforms fall into two categories: constraints on banks and constraints on borrowers. As far as the banks are concerned, market forces would have restrained excessive risk taking more effectively if banks had been required to disclose their international lending activity and if more adequate provisions had been made against the possibility of losses. The case for disclosure is a strong one, although it may not be prudent to move in this direction until international financial tensions have eased. Mandatory provisions, on the other hand, present formidable practical difficulties. Initially at any rate, regulatory authorities must be given considerable discretion with which to implement such provisions so that they do not interfere with other parts of the solution to the crisis. Finally, banks' capital resources should be strengthened to ensure that banks with the largest loans outstanding to developing countries have adequate capital backing.

Most important, a system needs to be set up to prevent banks from getting into a situation in which insolvency could result from the default of a single country. The most effective constraint would be a uniform country-lending limit, measured as a percentage of the lending bank's capital, with extended transitional arrangements designed to preclude any disruptive withdrawal of international credit. However, since many banks are already overextended, the proposal for capital-adequacy guidelines linked to concentrations of country exposure may be more feasible than lending limits.

Whatever proposals are adopted, regulatory agencies should be allowed broad discretion. In a rapidly changing economic environment in which short- and long-term considerations may conflict, specific legislative action would probably be too rigid. Agencies themselves should formulate regulatory guidelines; Congress should only monitor progress.

Constraints on borrowers are necessary, too. Because international credit markets lack the basic legal safeguards taken for granted in domestic lending operations, banks cannot impose conditions on many types of international lending and have little or no control over the level of a country's total external indebtedness. Therefore, bank creditors have had to rely on the self-restraint of foreign governments to ensure that the quality of outstanding loans is not eroded through excessive borrowing. Recent experience suggests, however, that foreign governments may be prepared to accumulate more debt than prudent banking standards dictate. Externally imposed constraints on the amount of bank debt that individual countries may incur would prevent this situation.

The IMF already specifies debt ceilings as a condition for some of its lending programs. To stabilize credit markets, it may be desirable to give continuous guidance to borrowers and lenders about appropriate levels of external debt. Although political and operational problems would have to be resolved, the IMF might be the appropriate body to enforce these guidelines, within its existing surveillance authority. This approach would contribute to a more stable international lending system.

Any lasting resolution of the debt crisis must strengthen the present emergency-lending regime, stabilize international credit markets over the long term, and ensure a prompt and sustained global economic recovery. Failure in any of these areas would further disturb international financial markets, with potentially damaging consequences for world trade and employment.